STACKING STONES

*A Testimony of
Hearing God
and Seeing
His Miracles*

Mark C. Connell

Stacking Stones

A Testimony of Hearing God and Seeing His Miracles

Mark C. Connell

ISBN (Print Edition): 978-1-66787-202-5

ISBN (eBook Edition): 978-1-66787-203-2

Some names have been changed because we were unable to reach them for name-use permission. All other names are published by expressly granted permission.

Written to my children

Contents

Welcome~

"Stacking Stones, A Testimony of Hearing God and Seeing His Miracles" was written for my children and my children's children! After I went through an experience with cancer in the Fall of 2016, the Lord said to me, "I want you to write down how I led you through this so your children will know." At the time, I agreed wholeheartedly. I did some journaling, but I had not written the whole testimony, nor given it to my kids. During the COVID lockdown in 2020, God asked me to start writing again. He started talking to me about different God moments in my life and to share as many as I could with my children. He wanted me to share with my kids the many ways their mom and I live with the Lord. And to tell them how the Lord has been intimately and intricately involved in our decisions~ sometimes as simple as what we say and do.

Stacking Stones was originally written for my three adult kids: my son, Stefen, and my daughters, Gracemarie and Jillienne. As I was writing the different God moment testimonies to my kids, I shared what I was doing with a few close friends and mentors. Quite a few people urged me, "Other people may benefit from your testimonies besides your children. It could be an encouragement to believers. You may want to publish that." One mentor said, "I think there might be a lot of people who would want to hear how God's led you and the different times He's spoken to you. Also, they may enjoy learning about the conversational intimacy you have with the Lord." So Jennifer and I prayed. We heard, "Yes. Write about me!" Months later in the Fall of 2021, after I had three surgeries in six weeks, I heard the Lord say, "I want you to finish that." So here we are!

If you are reading this and you are not one of my three children, please know the context of the writing will be specific to them or our family. I chose not to explain names and situations, as I would not normally do that with my children because they would know their grandmother's nickname so to speak. In a sense, you are reading personal stories much like journal entries. This insight will give you some context as you're reading. We named it Stacking Stones as a memorial and testimony to what God did in our lives much like in the book of Joshua. In the book of Joshua in the Bible, the Jewish people were going into the Promised Land and were able to cross the Jordan River on dry land. God instructed them to get one stone out of the Jordan per each tribe of Israel, then stack the stones up as a memorial.

I love the bible story because if you read that scripture closely, it says, "When your children ask in time to come, 'What do those stones mean to you?' then you shall tell them that the waters of the Jordan were cut off before the ark of the covenant of the Lord. So these stones shall be to the people of Israel a memorial forever." In a similar manner, when the "Stacking Stones" book is sitting on my children's, or grandchildren's coffee table or end table, their kids might ask, "What's that book about with the stones on the cover?" Stacking Stones would be a testimony of God in our lives, so our children and our grandchildren can learn about how we lived with God and God lived with us. That is the reason we wrote and bound the book~ and our hope is that it would be passed down to generations.

I pray that Stacking Stones would encourage you to pursue the Lord, to know that He does speak, He does heal, and that He has great things for you as you pursue Him, walk with Him, talk with Him and enjoy life with Him.

I offer this to you as a testimony of the Lord Jesus, the Heavenly Father, and the Holy Spirit in our lives. I hope that it blesses you as you read.

To my beautiful, amazing kids, I wrote this out of obedience to God for His stated purpose that you would KNOW HIM, and your children would know Him! Personally, I hope you would be inspired, and you would put God first in your life! My hope and prayer are that you may draw closer to the Lord Jesus, know that He is with you, around you, and speaking to you by the power of the Holy Spirit!

I pray this in Jesus' sweet and authoritative name.

You Will Need To Be Healthy

I'm sharing the testimony of how God led mom and me through the season of being diagnosed with cancer in September 2016. God is the one who has instructed me to share this with you kids so y'all know how He took care of us and moved in our lives mightily. There are quite a few things that happened along the way that we didn't disclose to you at the time because we were still walking through it and not sure how to process it ourselves.

Before I was diagnosed with cancer in September of 2016, I had an interesting encounter with the Lord in May of that year. In May, I was 49 years old staring down 50 on August 18th. What most people don't know is that I was dreading the day I turned 50. For some reason, I believed, "On my 50th birthday, I'm going to be officially old." So from my 49th birthday on, I lived in constant dread of turning 50. One morning in my alone time with the Lord in May of 2016, He said, "Hey, I need you to get in shape. I need you to get healthy because what I have for you in this next decade will require you to be healthy to do it." I excitedly replied, "Okay." I did my little Scooby Doo impression. My mind raced. I was thinking, "There's stuff to do in the next decade? What He has for me? Oh my gosh! That sounded exciting." I immediately started going to the rec center, working out, eating right, and running. God definitely shifted my thoughts from dreading the BIG FIVE- O, to being excited about it! I became proactive and very hopeful. Welp, I got healthy and turned 50 in August. The birthday was so much fun filled with family and friends. I felt good and healthy.

Three weeks later I was diagnosed with cancer.

On a Tuesday morning, in the second week of September, my testimony begins with a seemingly minor concern. I was having abdominal pain. Since I'd already had kidney stones before, I pretty much knew it was kidney stone pain. I told mom. We got up and went to the ER. They do all the CT scans, blood work, etc. Standard stuff. They confirmed, "Yeah, you have a kidney stone. You need to go see your urologist." We went to the urologist that same day. Mom went with me because I was in pain and it was difficult to walk. We visit and decide to have surgery Friday at 1p. The doc planned to do a sonar blast (which I had not done before) and blow up the kidney stone. I was thankful, "Great. Thumbs up. Awesome."

In that season, I was working as a pastor for the fourth-largest church in America. I was also studying for my Master's with classes on Friday mornings. It was Tuesday. So I let my professor know that I had kidney stone surgery scheduled for Friday, and I probably wouldn't make it to class. I had kidney stone surgery twice before so I know the drill. After Thursday night at midnight, I couldn't take food, water, etc. including pain meds. On the previous surgeries, I woke up the morning of surgery in severe pain. It was difficult to walk, difficult to move. When I woke up the Friday morning of surgery, I had no pain. I mean, no pain at all! Well, I had prayed and asked God to heal me. I rejoiced aloud, "I'm healed! I think I'm going to class!" Mom was shocked, "Really?" I confirmed, "Yeah. I feel fine. Maybe God healed me!"

To be on the safe side, I asked mom to drive me to class. Mom agreed. I went to class without any issues. Mom picked me up and we headed to the hospital for surgery. As we were going down highway 360 toward the hospital in Arlington, I kept thinking, "I feel fine." I started to question whether I needed to have the surgery. In my mind, I was wondering, "Oh my gosh, this could be super cool. God healed me. This would be great!"

We got to the hospital and the first thing I had to do is go to the restroom. So I go. Then it dawns on me that having a kidney stone makes it nearly impossible, or at the very least, unbearable to go to the restroom! Remember, it was a kidney stone. I came out of the restroom and thought to myself, "This sure seems like I'm good." I shared with mom how I felt and what was happening in my body. Mom was adamant about following the rules. She reminded me, "They have a surgery room waiting for you. They have nurses waiting for you. They have doctors that have allocated this time. They are preparing for surgery. You can't not show." I contended, "If I'm healed, I think I can not show. Why not? I mean like, why do I have to have surgery if I feel good?" She exhaled, "Oh my gosh." I implored her, "Hey, I feel like we need to pray about this. We ask God about so many other things. I want to go to the car and pray. Would you please come to the car and pray with me? And we'll ask God if I'm supposed to have this surgery."

Mom relented, "Okay."

We went to the car. We both began praying out loud, asking the Lord, "am I supposed to have this surgery?" I immediately heard, "No." I thought, "Let me wait for a second to see what mom gets." Mom looks up. I questioned, "What'd you hear?" She said, "I heard no." I replied, "Yeah, that's what I heard. No." Mom concluded, "Okay, I guess we're not doing the surgery." I literally called the hospital from the parking lot to cancel the surgery – like right then!!

I had no pain the rest of the weekend ~ until Tuesday.

Tuesday of the next week, I woke up with mild abdominal pain similar to kidney stone pain. I thought, "Oh my gosh, nooo! I thought I was healed." This time the pain wasn't so bad, so I drove myself to the ER and checked in by myself. They run the standard imaging and blood work. I'm in my own patient room sitting there by myself. The PA comes back and he flatly said, "Okay, so here's what you got. You have elevated pancreas enzymes, so we'd like to admit you to monitor those and see what that's about. You do have a kidney stone. Looks like you were scheduled for surgery. I'm not sure what happened with the surgery, but your kidney stone is still there. And then the mass that you have, I'm sure you've already talked about what you're going to do with that with your Urologist ." I queried, "Excuse me? What did you say? Mass?" He affirmed, "Well, mass, like tumor. I'm sure you've already had that conversation with your urologist since that was in last week's imaging." I challenged, "I don't know what you're talking about. Like tumor, like cancer tumor?" He confirmed, "Well, it could be, but I mean, you don't know for sure. I'm sure your Urologist covered that with you last week." I looked at him and I argued, "No. My doctor never talked to me about that. I don't know what you're talking about." He continued, "well, he probably talked to you about it last week. You might have been on meds or not paid attention." I said, "Nope. My wife was with me all day last Tuesday. Never left my side, not in this hospital nor at the doctor's offices because I could barely walk. I can assure you the C word never came up. I promise you, if my wife heard Cancer, we would have been talking about it. So, no. No one has ever said boo to me about having a cancer tumor. I have no idea what you're talking about!" That's when his demeanor changed. The PA's eyes got all wide and he blurted, "I'll be back."

He never came back. No one did. For over two hours.

Time seemed to stand still. I just sat on the cold table. I didn't move. Nothing seemed to move. The hum of the fluorescent lights above me sounded like something was moving, but it didn't. I had never really noticed that the room was so sterile. Metal tables, cabinets, and chairs. Gloves, wipes, and swabs are stacked orderly on the counter. Tiled walls. Even the floors were buffed and polished. Is the chilly air supposed to keep things sterile? "He should be back by now," I thought. My watch showed it had only been eight minutes. Even my thoughts were slow- like slowmo on a football playback reel. Then my thoughts raced. "Great. I could have cancer. Oh my gosh, what does that mean? Oh my God." I thought about everything and everyone who meant something to me. I thought about mom, and all the places we wanted to go. I thought about you kids~ graduations, weddings, grandchildren. At some point, I broke down and had a quiet cry thinking of the things which may not come. I processed quite a bit. I took some deep breaths to calm down, then called mom. I asked mom if a tumor was mentioned the week before and she said no. We prayed and hung up. Then I waited for someone to come- for the longest two hours of my life.

When a doctor did come in, he proceeded to assure me, "I'm confident your doctor talked to you about this last week." I contended, "No, he didn't. I mean, it's not a big deal. I'm saying it didn't happen. Now, what's the next step?" He replied, "We're going to admit you for your pancreas enzymes and probably schedule you for kidney stone surgery in the morning. And I guess you can figure out with your doctor what you want to do about your tumor, your mass." I said, "Okay."

I was admitted to the hospital. My urologist did show up later that day because he was going to do my kidney stone surgery. When he came in, he is chatting me up, "Hey, how are ya?" I interrupted, "Hey, you never told me about the mass. What is that about?" He was acting as if he did tell me when he didn't. We got into it a little bit. I finally demanded, "Hey, that didn't happen and you know it." He eventually backed down and apologized for the mishap. I didn't want to argue about it. I wanted to know what to do about it.

The next morning, my urologist did the kidney stone surgery WITHOUT a sonar blast on my kidney stone. Later that day, the floor doctor was checking on me, "Hey, you're the patient that said the doctor never told you about your cancer tumor." I offered, "Well, he didn't." The floor doctor made a comment "it sounds like you want retribution or revenge". I explained, "Hey, this has nothing to do with retribution revenge, or anything. In my faith, you settle your disputes before you go to court. It's not about taking anybody to court or any problems like that. That didn't happen and that's wrong. That's all I'm saying. And especially if you guys think it is important to let someone know he may have cancer." He listened and then left the room. A couple of hours later right before I was discharged, a nurse comes in with a sealed manila envelope. She said, "Dr. so and so wanted you to have this. This is private and you didn't get it from him." I replied, "Okay."

When we left and got to the car, we opened the envelope.

It was a computer printout of doctor's note entries about me. Each entry had a timestamp and the doctor was entering the information. It showed the radiologist's entry the prior week about the mass. It showed that my urologist had put in notes about me the prior week regarding the kidney stone, but does not list any notes about the mass/tumor. However, it showed that the urologist did enter a note the evening that I returned to the ER and was checked into the hospital, stating that he talked with me the week before. Looks like someone was attempting to cover his tracks! SMH…

Why is any of this important?

Because the sonar blast designed to blow up a tiny but very hard kidney stone would have blown up my cancer tumor and spread cancer over my entire body. And I probably wouldn't be here today. It could've been fatal. God told mom and me not to have the surgery to SAVE MY LIFE! Had God not ordered our steps, I would not be here today.

Next step: we began to get opinions on cancer treatment.

At the first cancer doctor we visited, everything was leather and gorgeous. I felt like I walked into a nice country club. They even assigned us a liaison who brought us drinks and snacks! It was the royal treatment. Since mom and I both had been in professional sales, we were aware of salesmanship and presentation, so our radars were up. We met with a kidney cancer doctor who literally spent 50 minutes describing himself, his background, his expertise, and what the procedure entailed- which was removing a whole kidney. It was a very long and drawn-out explanation. All the while, we were being waited on hand and foot by our liaison giving us coffee, snacks, and water bottles. We were getting schmoozed- Big Time. It was both interesting and unsettling to experience.

We leave, and before we even get to the car, Mom quizzes, "So what did you think about that?" I complained, "I felt like we were getting 'sold'." She completely agreed. Y'all know mom and I have had some very comfortable days in our life- been country club members, nice cars, been around millionaires, even a billionaire, etc.- so the schmoozing part wasn't going to impact our decision in choosing a doctor. If anything, it put our radar up. I wanted a great doctor, not a great presentation. Also, his solution was to take out the whole kidney, not just the cancer tumor in the kidney. We went home and started to pray about what to do next.

We felt led to get a second opinion, so I posted on Facebook to see if anyone I knew could give me a recommendation. People gave me names and referrals for a reputable research hospital in Dallas and a cancer research hospital in Houston. We went to see the doctor in Dallas first. From start to finish, our appointment was seven minutes. He came in and flatly explained, "This is what you have. This is what we do. This is how we handle it. It will be difficult, but I do difficult every day. My guess is you wouldn't have come to see me if it wasn't difficult. Any questions?" It was straight up BALLA! It was greatness. Yes, that's what I want! In. Out. Swagger. It's hard. I can do it. No problem. By the way, the reason it was difficult was the tumor was sitting on the main vein or an artery. One question I had was about the reason that the other doctor wanted to remove the whole kidney versus the tumor only. His response was golden, "Well, that would be the easiest thing to do. We don't do easy. We do difficult, and I do difficult every day. Don't worry about it. I can do it." He added, "one of the things we have learned in the last 10 to 20 years is that it's best to leave as much of your kidney intact."

What a great appointment!

Next, we headed down to Houston to see another excellent doctor. Guess what? Same thing. I think this appointment was nine minutes. He casually explained, "You have this. We would do this. We would do that. Deet. Deet. Deet. It's difficult. I can do it." I was so comforted to see super reputable, world-renowned doctors did not sugarcoat it. Shoot it straight. Tell it like it is. What else do you need to know? We discussed the next appointment choices and left. It was that fast. It was super great. And I mean, the information at both research hospitals was identical which was very comforting. On the way home, as I prayed and thought about it, I shared with mom, "Since they both said the same thing, I prefer the doctor in Dallas. It allows the family to be there without causing anyone to travel." We both prayed about it and felt like that was the best decision.

While we are going through all the physical steps to address the physical aspects of the cancer, I was also going through the spiritual steps to address the spiritual aspects of the cancer.

I had been praying and praying against the spirit of infirmity. Y'all have probably heard me talk about the 14 demons named in the Bible. One of the named demons is the spirit of infirmity. The scripture also holds that we've been granted all authority in Christ to overcome the work and the power of the enemy. It's the authority delegated by Jesus to us so we can operate with His authority over those demons. Knowing this, I had been praying against and taking authority over the spirit of infirmity on a daily basis since I was diagnosed.

When we went in for another checkup in October, the doctors shared that the tumor is still there— I still have cancer. I was very frustrated, "ugh." The next night after all y'all had gone to bed, I'm talking with the Lord about permissions and intrusion regarding the spirit of infirmity working in my body. The word of God reflects two ways that the enemy attacks us. The one way is through intrusion, which means he does not have permission to be there. We can pray against it and he'll flee. The second way the enemy attacks us is through permission. Meaning we grant the enemy permission to wreak havoc in our lives through willful sin, vows, and agreements, unforgiveness, and judgment, hurts/traumas, and curses. I had been praying and taking authority over the spirit of infirmity, but it didn't go away. I had a gut check that night. I'm thinking, "well, if I believe that I have delegated authority, the flip side of taking authority over intrusion is that I may have given permission." I didn't think I had any permissions granted to the enemy. But I went ahead and asked, "Lord, do I have any open doors where I've given permission to the enemy to wreak havoc in my life?" Very gently. Very kindly. And very quietly, I heard, "Yeah. You do." I was stunned, "Really?" Gently, He continued, "You have unforgiveness, you have bitterness, you have some anger."

I wept.

I didn't know. I didn't know that at all. Then the Lord started showing me all the different people that I had unforgiveness, bitterness, and offenses toward. He showed me each one, like replaying events in my mind – most I had forgotten. He showed me that some of the people whom I had unforgiveness or offenses towards had not done anything to me. They had done things toward people that I knew. Due to my role as a biblical counseling pastor, I would visit with staff who sometimes shared things that happened at work. Some of the situations the Lord revealed were not things that happened to me. They were offenses that someone had committed against someone else, but I had picked up their offense unwittingly. Then I held onto it. Then forgot it. It was as if I packed something in my backpack, forgot about it, but then carried the weight of it around with me. And if you would have asked me two weeks before if I had any of these, I would have answered, "No, I'm good." But that night, the Lord was showing me places in my heart where unforgiveness, bitterness, offenses, and anger had rooted. I wept dearly as He revealed each situation. I mean, I'm bawling. My heart is undone. I cried out, "Oh, I'm so sorry. I'm so sorry. I don't want that."

I then remembered that I actually know what needs to happen for me to close those doors of permission. I hate to say it, but I love to say it—that's what I do for a living! I help people close those doors and revoke the permissions they have granted to the enemy. The spiritual realm works in authority. When we grant lawful permission to the enemy to steal, wreak havoc, and destroy, it's also within our authority to revoke it! It's a lot like signing a lease or a contract. It is permitted under the law. We have allowed them permission in our house and they're not going to leave until we remove their legal authority, revoke permissions, and evict them! If you look at scripture, authority is all through the Word of God. It is how it works. While I knew how to walk through it, it takes some time to walk through each situation the Lord revealed. Over the following days, the Lord kindly walked me through each situation. He even revealed what some folks were working through and how He is not "done with them yet." He didn't have to show me anything that person was working on, but He did. In doing so, the Lord helped me to have compassion and grace toward them. The next several days walking through these situations were tender, holy, and incredibly intimate times with the Lord.

The next week in my alone time with God, I heard the Lord say, "I'm going to heal you". I was so overwhelmed with joy and peace, "Whoa, this is awesome. I'm super excited." I know people who were healed of physical ailments. Grammy was healed of her borderline cirrhosis of the liver. She was also healed of having to use a CPAP machine. Jillienne, you had your eyesight healed. I've met other healed people at church also. In a step of faith, I let everyone know, "the Lord told me He is going to heal me. Would you please agree with me in prayer that God's going to do what he said?!"

We had one final MRI appointment before the scheduled surgery. I was hoping to hear that I was healed!

The final MRI was scheduled for early morning so we could review it with the doctor that same day at 4:30 pm. On my drive to my final MRI, as I'm singing and worshipping in the car, the Lord brought to my memory a Bible study I attended about 12 years earlier. The study explained the three different provisions which God gives for healing. I remembered the three. The first provision God gives for healing is "natural healing." He created the body to heal itself. You cut yourself, the body starts working on it immediately. It scabs up and starts to regenerate. Right? The second provision is "supernatural healing." This is what most of us consider when we hear, "Oh, someone was healed." The third provision God gives for healing is through His wisdom He grants to people. God grants wisdom to humans. He gives them giftings and abilities to be doctors and researchers. It's a God-given gift. As soon as I remembered that Bible study, I started laughing. I knew God brought that to my mind because he was going to heal me through doctors. I just knew it. I thanked Him, "You know what, God? I am super cool being healed by doctors! I am absolutely fine with that. Thank you. Thank you for this sweet moment of memory. I love how you love me. You're so sweet. And thank you." I continue to the MRI and complete it that morning.

I meet mom back up at the doctor's office that afternoon.

From the doctor's perspective, this appointment was to detail the final steps of "how" they would perform the procedure. For us, it was the final appointment to confirm God's healing~ except I felt the Lord already informed me that morning how I would be healed. We arrive and were seated in the doctor's office. The doctor we met with before came in. He is sitting a bit to my left. Mom is sitting to my right. So we're sitting angled in the chairs leaning our heads and vision to our left. I can't see mom at all. She's almost behind me to my right. The doctor begins, "Hey, we looked at your final MRI images. Here's the deal. It's not as difficult as would require my skills. The final MRI revealed that we will be able to do it with robotics. And the doctor that does the robotics is someone else. It's not me. I'm gonna go get him. Then, we'll talk about it." Our doc leaves and returns with the new doc. The new doc comes in and starts talking with us, "Here's the situation. The tumor is this, the tumor is that. It's still there. Sitting right on a main artery... and we're going to do this, this, and this... "

Then he said, "Do you need to talk about it?" I replied, "What? No, I don't need to talk about it. Let's go. Let's schedule this." He quizzed, "Okay. Well, how soon would you like to do it?" I suggested, "As soon as possible. Geez, I've been living with this since September. Let's get to schedule, how fast can you do it?" The doctor offers, "Well you have time. I mean, you can talk about it and think about it if you want." I pushed, "No, I don't want to talk about it or think about anything. Just schedule, let's do this! I'm absolutely completely ready." Then he said, "well," and paused. I had never detected any hesitation or pause from these doctors until now. I didn't know what was going on. I mean, every time I talked with the doctors or people down at this research hospital, they have been very direct, candid, and quick to make decisions. So when he paused, there was something in his eyes I could not quite make out in the moment. He continued, "I tell you what? Why don't y'all talk about it first? I'll be back." And he leaves the room. I thought, "What is going on?" After he leaves, I turned to look at mom. Mom was quiet crying. Big tears were coming down her face.

I mean, she was crying. But no sound.

I didn't even know it because I couldn't see her by the way we were seated. The poor doctors were trying to give me hints. Through her tears, mom lamented, "I thought God said He was going to heal you." Ugh. I had forgotten to tell mom about my "car moment" with the Lord that morning; and the three different provisions for healing. I apologized and proceeded to give her my complete experience from the car that morning and that I believe that God will heal me through surgery.

It was a tough moment emotionally for both of us. Obviously, I felt horrible that I hadn't told mom what happened earlier that day. And mom's expectations of the tumor being removed supernaturally left her disheartened a bit. When the doctors came back in, they added one more clear message of hope and healing: "If the surgery goes well, you won't need any radiation or any chemotherapy." WHOA! Astounding news!

I had the surgery. It went well. I had no chemo, no radiation, and that was the short of it.

The really amazing thing is if I didn't have a relationship where I'm walking and talking with God, I may have had the original surgery blowing up the tumor! And of course, the way God allowed me to have no pain which led me to skip the surgery was miraculous as well. The ways that God moved in my life to deliver me from cancer and potential death, and deliver me from a doctor who didn't have his "A" game is humbling. God was merciful to me and to all of y'all as He brought me through cancer. It was a surreal and memorable time in my life. It was hard as well, yet spiritually intimate, beautiful, and holy. I think it is a great testimony of how God moves~ some things He did were counter to my understanding. Like when He said, "I'm going to heal you." Mom and I thought it would be supernaturally. Yet, He reminded us that there are other ways to be healed! I certainly had to think about death and the what-ifs when I first heard the word cancer-those things cross your mind. I thought about each one of you, what would I do? What would life be like? I mean, as a dad, I love being a dad and I love each one of you so much, and I enjoy you. I want to be with you. I'm so grateful to God that He poured His mercy on me. I also feel like He poured His mercy on y'all that you didn't have to deal with your dad's death at a very young age. I'm really, really grateful.

God has asked me to share this with you so you can know that He is real. He is merciful. He is loving. He is faithful. He will talk to you. He will guide you. He will lead you. If you pursue Him and let Him, He wants to be close to you and to walk with you. God has sweet, intimate, good things for each one of you. I love each one of you so much. And I'm so grateful that I've had all the years past 2016 to be with you and to enjoy the holy, incredibly fun, and tough times together as a family. God wanted you to know this. This was my experience in 2016, and it was amazing. I thank God for the opportunity to live life each day with a little more gratitude than before. I love y'all.

Bless you~

MY PRAYER FOR YOU:

I pray that you would walk and talk with the Lord. I pray that you would trust yourself in hearing the "God pauses" in your life. I pray you would realize that our physical, spiritual, and emotional lives are intertwined and that they affect each other. I pray each of you would know that I am imperfect, flawed, and full of love for you! And that God loves you WAAAY more than I do! (which I cannot fully understand, but it's true!)

I Can Do All Things Through Christ Who Strengthens Me

This testimony happened when Gracemarie was around three years old. She was a toddler and had come down with RSV. RSV caused her to lose bodily fluids which made her very listless. Since Gracemarie was born with four heart abnormalities, RSV was a serious matter because it taxed her heart. To be dehydrated was a serious situation for Gracemarie, so she was admitted to a hospital in Plano.

Gracemarie was faint, listless, and had become incoherent. She was sleeping constantly. Due to the lack of fluids, the hospital hooked her up to an IV. As a parent, the situation was pretty stressful. I was freaking out and having a difficult time. I told mom I needed a break and went downstairs to the first floor. The hospital had a big open lobby area with couches. I found a newspaper and sat on a couch up against a wall. I put the newspaper up high enough to where no one could see my face. And then I wept~ a kind of quiet cry. The one thing that kept going through my head over and over was, "I can't do this. I can't do this. I can't do this." If something happened to Gracemarie, or if she passed away. No way. All I could think of was, "I can't do this. I can't do this. I can't do this, God." I could not think of anything else. It's the only thought that came to my mind. Over and over and over for close to 30 minutes. It was a constant, "I can't do this." That and crying.

When I regained my composure, I put the newspaper down and decided to go back up to the room.

The room had a bed that Gracemarie was sleeping in and another chair/bed combo where we slept the night before. When I got back to the hospital room, one of the hospital staff walked in to change the bed sheets. She asked if I would move Gracemarie from her bed to the bed that we had slept in the night before. "Happy to," I replied. I stepped to Gracemarie's bed. Then gently, I lift Gracemarie in my arms. I carefully navigated the short distance and gingerly laid her tiny little body down on our bed. The moment her body rested on the bed, Gracemarie opened her eyes and turned her head to me. She looked straight into my eyes and said, "I can do all things through Christ who strengthens me." Then she slowly turned her head back to the bed and closed her eyes. I lost it and burst into uncontrollable tears. Mom blurted, "What happened? What happened?" "She talked." "Oh my gosh, she talked!" The medical staff started scrambling around to see if Gracemarie was coherent, but she wasn't. Prior to this moment, Gracemarie hadn't talked for a day or more. She had been completely out of it. And in an instant, Gracemarie had gone back to sleep!

I knew God had done some type of miraculous moment or a God moment of speaking to me. How does a three-year-old even know that scripture? And why would she speak it right then? I had never heard Gracemarie say that verse before. Mom never heard her say that verse before. Neither Mom nor I had taught her that verse. And let me tell you, I was absolutely undone. No more quiet crying for me. I cried uncontrollably and could not talk. The floodgate had opened and the tears were flowing. Of course, I was freaking out too! I'm the only one that knew what was going on in my head downstairs in the lobby. Mom was still wondering the reason I was so emotional. I was finally able to calm down. I explained to mom what happened downstairs and what was going down in my head. We were both in awe and we knew something huge had just happened.

I can't fully explain the moment and how it felt to be completely known, exposed, and encouraged all at the same time. I was in shock for quite a while after that moment. I will always remember her sweet little face looking up at me and saying, "I can do all things through Christ, who strengthens me." It was so awesome! Gracemarie recovered later that day and we went home from the hospital. I always remember that verse anytime I feel like I can't do something.

Love y'all.

MY PRAYER FOR YOU:

I pray that you will realize that God is speaking, communicating, and involved in your life right now. I pray that God can and will help you when you don't think you can do something. I pray that you will know that coincidences could just be GOD reaching out to you. I pray you will fully grasp that you can do all things through Christ who strengthens you!

Those Who Teach

I want to share this next God testimony because it was a transforma-
tional moment in my spiritual life. It was at a time when I wasn't
convinced that God could and did talk to us. The testimony starts at
church. Y'all know that sometimes I would teach in the youth group
bible classes. One summer, I was teaching the kids who were leaving
6th grade and would be in the Youth Group in the Fall as 7th graders.
I was teaching a class about the different types of relationships God
created. To make it fun and engaging, we invited some of the kids to
act out the relationship they were going to learn and talk about that
day. While a few kids were acting it out, the remaining class would
guess what relationship was being portrayed. Fun, engaging, and visual!
Each week was different. One week came when the relationship was
between God and people. Before class, I had a couple of the kids out
in the hallway who was going to act it out. One of them asked, "Hey,
can I get up and stand on the table to be God?" I agreed, "Sure." We
briefly talked about what the skit would look like. It was always a pretty
quick and simple performance. They went in, acted it out, and within
a minute or two the kids would guess what it is. This week, one of the
kids was going to silently stand on the table with his arms crossed. A
couple of other kids would be down at the table on their knees praying
to God. God never answered. He did not speak. The kids picked up on

what the relationship was almost immediately. So that was the introduction to that week's lesson on a relationship with God~ that God doesn't actually respond in a way we would hear and know it was Him. At the end of class, I told the kids, "Hey, next weekend, I'm going to be out of town on a deep-sea fishing trip. I have a substitute coming in."

I had never been deep-sea fishing before.

I was invited to the deep-sea fishing trip by a good friend of mine named Jeff. One of his buddies from college, and another good friend of mine named Rory were going as well. Four of us in all. These guys are big, strong guys. Rory wrestled in college. Jeff is like 6'4", I think. Ron is also like 6'4" or thereabouts. These guys were big strong men that I was going to go deep-sea fishing with. I was looking forward to the trip! The boat we were going out on was like a 65-foot boat. It's no small boat. It had three levels. They had done this many times before and kept their boat down in the Freeport/Lake Jackson area of the Texas coast. We were going to head down on Friday. Go out all day Saturday and Sunday. Then drive back Sunday night.

We went down to Lake Jackson on Friday as planned. Saturday morning we get up and out on the boat, shoving off about 8:00 AM. Soon after leaving the dock, we had an odd weather experience. The winds kicked up in such a way as to cause the exhaust to keep blowing right back at us on the boat. The boat had two big diesel engines. I started to get nauseous. Within 30 minutes of departing the dock, I'm vomiting. Not a good start. Not long after that, I had an odd thought in my head, "put your lifejacket on." I looked around and nobody else has a life jacket on. I had the thought again, 'put your life jacket on.' I thought to myself, "I don't know if that's a God thing or I'm talking to myself, but okay." (I tend to trust myself if I have some thoughts.) I get a lifejacket and start to put it on. Immediately, my buddies started to razz me, as good friends do. No biggie. Looking back, it was the first clue of what was about to come. We kept going out into the Gulf of Mexico. Dark clouds moved in about 9a and the sky started getting really dark. The wind picked up even more. I asked the guys, "Hey you guys, if a storm comes, do we turn back?" They bragged, "Well, of all the years we've been doing this, we've only turned back once." I accepted, "Oh, okay." They continued, "Man, it was practically a hurricane was the only reason we turned back. We're probably not going to turn back. It's only windy and overcast." I'm like, "Okay, that's cool," because I really wanted to get the deep-sea fishing experience!

The boat has three levels and sleeps six. The sleeping cabin is the lowest level. Above that is the command deck. The top level is a lookout/seating deck.

I had climbed up to the command deck where Jeff was steering the boat as the storm began to worsen. The waves started coming up and hitting the command deck which is about 10-15 feet above water level. The waves eventually worsened to 30-foot swells. I had never seen such a sight in my life. I was getting nervous for sure. I was holding on to the railing of the boat, so when we went up and over a wave, I'd be airborne. Then BOOM, we'd hit the water and I'd hit the bench! It was getting super painful and a little scary. One big concern was that each time we went over a huge wave, the boat transom would land IN the water first, take on water, then level out. This was happening over and over – and the boat was taking on water.

I started praying that the waves would stop and that the storm would die down and go away. I remembered a bible study mom had just finished. The leader encouraged believers to pray God's word back to God in agreement with Him. I was thinking of scripture to pray back to God and doing that in the midst of the crazy storm. The crashing of the waves and the rushing wind was so noisy that we couldn't hear each other very well without screaming. It was pure chaos and Jeff was courageously navigating us through it. At one point, an alarm started going off, "Woo, woo, woo, woo." It was some sort of safety beacon that was going off which added to the chaos. I'm telling you, it was crazy and stressful. I yelled towards Jeff, "Hey, are we going to turn back?" He hollered over the crashing waves, "No, but you need to pray." I laughed out loud and encouraged him, "I'm already praying!" Rory was standing with Jeff at the controls at this moment when the next wave hit us. When the boat hit the water, it jolted in an awkward way and knocked Rory into the command console with the steering wheel and the engine levers. Rory landed on one of the engine levers. He knocked the lever straight down and snapped the lever clean off! It killed one engine immediately. The look in Jeff's eyes when that happened was serious fear. It was like, oh snap! This is so not good. Now you only have one engine working. Jeff found some vice grips but the engine lever was snapped off so close to the base that the vice grips could not get hold of the engine lever.

"MAY-DAY! MAY-DAY!" Jeff made the call. I knew it was serious now. And I knew Jeff knew it was serious.

Jeff and I had met at church in bible class. Y'all know that Jeff and I also attended the same Life Group together with mom and his wife Gloria. Our wives got along like sisters. Jeff and I even did business together. He loved and played with y'all girls as if y'all were his own. He was a defender of people he loved, and cared deeply for others. I loved him like a brother. And I trusted him like a brother. So when he knew it was serious, I believed him. Jeff turned the boat around and headed for shore.

It was approximately 9:30a.

I looked down below at the lower deck and I couldn't see Rory and didn't see him go into the sleep cabin area. I didn't know what happened to him. I was hoping he went into the cabin and didn't go overboard. None of these guys had life jackets on at this point. I began asking the Lord to stop the waves and stop the storm. Suddenly, I heard, "I won't stop the storm." My first instinct was to say, "Get behind me Satan!" I pleaded with God, "Please stop the storm. Please stop all of this. This is crazy." I heard, "I won't stop the storm because they won't turn back." I was baffled, "Huh?" It was a very strange moment for me because this conversation began in the midst of all the chaos, noise, and wind. And the voice did not seem harsh, evil, or mean, yet it did not make any sense to me. I finally spoke directly to the voice, "am I going to be alright?" I heard, "Yes." The moment I heard "yes", I had a deep, consuming, and surreal peace come over me that I cannot explain. I knew that I was going to be alright – meaning, I would live. Total calm. All fear had left. Total peace. No stress. At this point, I believed the voice to be God. I asked God, "Well, can I go below"? (I had seen enough cable TV shows to know when a boat capsizes and flips upside down, people who are caught in the cabin area are sucked down with the boat and can't get out- so I was not about to go down below.) God gently encouraged me, "Yes." I went below.

When I entered the cabin area of the boat, I saw Rory.

Rory was laid flat across the entrance to the sleeping area of the boat completely passed out, laying left to right. He had vomited everywhere. I thought, "Oh my God, Lord." He had no lifejacket on. I tried to close the door but couldn't. I stepped over him, went in, got in a bunk, and slept. They woke me up three hours later when we reached the dock. The boat took three hours to get back to the dock. I kid you not, I slept the whole way back. They even have a picture of me in my bunk with my life jacket on, sleeping like a baby. It was amazing, horrific, bizarre, and surreal.

Here is the confirmation for me that God spoke to me and saved us all.

As soon as we got back to the dock, Jeff had gone into the hull of the boat. When he went below, the water in the hull of the boat was up to the top of his chest, almost to his chin. Recall, Jeff is 6'5". He's a big guy. What does that mean? BOTH bilge pumps were not working. The bilge pump alarms never went off which would have let them know the pumps were not working! Bilge pumps remove the water that gathers in the hull of a boat. The bilge pump alarms are supposed to go off when the bilge pumps are inoperable or working incorrectly. Remember, we were going to go 3-5 hours into the Gulf of Mexico, fish all day, then come back. We would have gone out into the Gulf of Mexico, taken on water, and never known until it was too late. We probably would have slowly sunk in the Gulf of Mexico with no one around, and not much opportunity for rescue. We could have died.

When we all realized the bilge bump situation, we were stunned. It just added to the exhaustion. It was also a very sobering moment. I thought, "Oh my God. You saved our life by allowing some massive storm to come up. I absolutely heard you. I had a God moment. Oh my gosh, this is nuts. Like, I cannot believe that God talked to me." I'm thinking, "it happened. There is no way around it. I had this moment." As I was processing this, I wanted to sit on land. After cleaning the boat, I got to the grass near the marina and sat for about 20 minutes. A light bulb went off in my mind, "I had a completely amazing moment with God which absolutely contradicts what I taught the kids the week before."

I hopped in the suburban and drove straight home from Lake Jackson that day. I called my mom and my dad on the way back, telling them I love them through my tears. It was a life-altering moment. While driving, James 3:1 came to mind which says, "teachers will be judged more strictly." When I heard that scripture, I thought, "Oh my gosh, I have to correct the record that God can and does speak." He clearly spoke in the Old Testament, the New Testament, and continues today." I knew I had to go back and tell the kids what I experienced. And I did.

I went to class the next morning. The kids questioned, "What are you doing here, Mr. Connell?" I began, "Well, I have something important to tell you. Y'all have a seat." It was the most silent the kids have ever been. Normally, they were some rambunctious, fun-loving, great kids. It wasn't like they were mean-spirited or disrespectful, but they had never been silent. That Sunday morning when I told them what happened to me, you could have heard a pin drop in the room. It was completely silent. I told them everything that happened with the storm, the conversation with God, what He said to me, how that played out, the peace, the sleep, James 3:1. The entire experience.

I never experienced God in that way before. I absolutely believe God allowed me to have that experience so I would set the record straight. He knows me. I'm pretty bold. He knows I am also willing. He knew I would go and set the record straight. And I did. That was the beginning of my eyes and ears being open to the possibility that God would actually speak to me and lead me and guide me. It opened my mind and heart to the possibility that I could talk intimately with God every day. Years later at graduations, weddings, and funerals, quite a few parents have thanked me and shared with me that their kids still talk about that day "Mr. Connell told them about God speaking" and how it changed their lives for the better!

MY PRAYER FOR YOU:

I pray you realize that sometimes a difficult storm that you can and do survive is ultimately designed to save your life. I pray you would not limit God when you teach about God. I pray you see that much of the Bible is a series of stories of all kinds of different people from all walks of life where God is present! I pray you will talk with God daily and listen intently to His voice.

I Already Healed You

Hey, y'all. This next God moment testimony has to do with my dad and my understanding of salvation, forgiveness, and inner healing. I believe it was in May of 2008. I was at an Advanced Boot Camp event up in Colorado. The camps go from Thursday to Sunday and are filled with a lot of healing, a lot of teaching, and training. Each day, participants were able to choose to go through inner healing ministry- if they wanted to.

I was resistant to participating in this because I was leery of what might come out. Y'all know I've survived some tough situations and painful events. On Saturday night, I went and did some inner healing "work" regarding my dad and some of my father wounds. I had so much unforgiveness towards my dad for so many different things. Lots of bad memories filled with deep emotions. When I was 10 years old, my dad literally came up and pulled me out of a baseball game when I was a pitcher, while I was on the pitcher's mound! He pulled me out of the football league championship game when I was 13, while I was in the huddle- screaming that he would "Come get me out of the huddle if I didn't come out". He left me at school. He didn't pick me up. He left me in jail. He left me all over the place. There are all sorts of father wounds that I had. I was scared of him my whole childhood in many ways. He was an angry man and led by fear and violence.

So I was working through father wounds on Saturday night ministry time. The ministry time was surprisingly amazing. I wasn't sure if I was going to be able to forgive him and get through the things that had happened, but I did. It was pretty cool. One significant point in the ministry process included the moment when I asked God if He would give me a word for how He sees my dad. I heard the word "ravaged." I knew my dad had a tumultuous upbringing. I knew he was in the military, served in Vietnam War, and had seen some tough stuff. I knew he had nightmares and slept on his stomach in a protective posture. The word "ravaged" gave me a sense of what my father had endured in his life which enabled me to have compassion toward him. It was a wonderful experience. I forgave him. I released him. I felt like the Lord healed me, and it was just so awesome.

Later that night at almost midnight, I got into my top bunk bed. I closed my eyes, ready to go to sleep. I told God, "Thank You so much for finally healing me tonight." Immediately I heard, "I already healed you." My eyes opened wide. I mean, it was dark, but I opened my eyes super wide. Stunned, I blurted out, "What?" He affirmed, "I already healed you when I saved you. It wasn't until tonight that you were willing to release your unforgiveness, anger, and vengeance toward your dad." I just burst into tears. As I cried, I processed what the Lord told me. Every bit of that is scriptural. Yes. The Bible states that we're healed by his stripes, so when we're saved, we're healed. It was hard to fathom in my mind, but He was right. I'd been saved for over a decade. I mean, it wasn't until that night I finally decided to release my dad. To confess my unforgiveness. To release my dad and pray blessings over him. Wow, that was super cool that God healed me and my heart when I was saved, but I finally chose to receive the healing 13 years later! What a lesson! It was huge. I just laid in bed and cried myself to sleep that night, at the tender age of 42.

I just wanted to share that Testimony with y'all because we are all saved. Yet there may be something that you're holding on to either towards me or mom or towards an old friend or someone that's hurt you. I hope that you'll be willing to release any person of your unforgiveness, of any vengeance, of any recourse that you have towards them, and that you'll be able to receive the fullness of God's healing in your life as soon as you possibly can and not wait decades into your forties as I did!

MY PRAYER FOR YOU:

I pray and ask you to forgive me for the pain and heartache I've caused you. I am flawed and broken. I've had bad dad moments in your life for sure! I pray you will draw close to the Lord so that you may release unforgiveness, anger, and vengeance against anyone in your life. I pray you will get to walk in the fullness of God's peace and joy by releasing anyone who has hurt you.

Take The Client

This testimony happened in a season when I was beginning to follow God, trying to hear His voice and doing what He asked me to do. The testimony I want to share with you was how I transitioned to working with the law firm. Y'all may remember that I owned two concurrent and complementary firms serving business owners. One business was a Registered Investment Advisory firm managing business owner investments. The other business was a bookkeeping, accounting, and CFO services firm which also served business owners. One day, a law firm in my office tower approached me to help them with their bookkeeping services. Here's the challenge: they were a law firm, and I never did business with law firms or attorneys. It was a business practice that I put in place years earlier. I refused to do business with attorneys because most I knew were relatively arrogant and difficult to work with. I reasoned, that if they wanted to sue you or threaten to sue you, they could do it easily without having to hire an attorney. I, on the other hand, would have to spend $300 or $400 an hour to hire an attorney. It seemed to me that they would be less incented to work things out, so I didn't like the relational imbalance. I never did business with attorneys all the years that I owned my own businesses. When the law firm reached out to me, I decided to pray about it. I heard, 'take the client'. I argued with God a little bit. I informed Him, "Well, I don't do business with attorneys. What do you think?" I heard, "take the client." Each time I prayed about it, I heard 'take the client.' I talked with God about this for about a week in my alone time. Each conversation revealed one thing: "take the client."

So I asked mom.

"Hey, Jen. Would you be willing to pray about this situation and ask God if I need to take this client? I was approached by a business in the office tower that I'm in." She queried, "Well, did you already ask God?" I replied, "Yeah." She quizzed me further, "Well, what'd he tell you?" "Take the client". "Well, why are you asking me then if you've already asked him," with an incredulous look on her face. I confessed, "Well, I guess I wasn't too keen on his answer." Mom gives me that look that only she can give, "Why aren't you doing it?" I admitted, "Well, it's a law firm. And you know I don't do business with lawyers." Mom nodded understandably, "Okay. I'll pray." Mom prayed for about a week, and heard the same thing, "take the client".

I was more than a little disappointed with that answer. But the next week, I sent the law firm a proposal for the work they requested. They countered the bid at the rate that I was paying my bookkeeper! This violated another business tenet I lived by, which was "how you enter into a relationship is generally a good understanding of how that relationship will go the rest of the time you do business with them". If I have someone upfront that is trying to get everything in the absolute cheapest way and leaves no room for reasonable profits, I won't do business with them.

To recap, they are attorneys. After the first proposal, they counter to a price point where I would make no profit. Obviously, I'm in business to make money. So I go back and talk to the Lord, "Seriously, God? What do you think about that?" He said, "Take the client." I contended, "God, that makes no sense to me. I'm in business. I have a wife. I have kids. I have bills to pay. Why would you instruct me to take a client where no profit would be earned? That makes no sense to me at all." I asked, "what do you think about that?" I heard "take the client". "UGGHHH." Let me tell you, I was super frustrated. And getting angry. I asked mom to pray again. We both heard the same thing. Reluctantly, I went ahead and took the client.

We had the client for about a month when one day, the two partners showed up at my office unannounced. No appointment. Just showed up. My assistant announced, "Hey, the attorneys are in our foyer." At that moment I remember thinking, "Well, this is just like attorneys. They're pushy, demanding, and arrogant. They think they can show up anytime they want." All that rushed through my mind. But things were going fine with the account otherwise. We were taking care of them, and reorganizing things in their bookkeeping, billing, and accounting. I decided, "You know what? Yeah, go ahead and have them come in. I'll take a break from the portfolio I was working on."

They come in and have a seat, "Hey, we want to talk with you." "Sure, what's up?" I asked. "We heard from your bookkeeper, that you do more than bookkeeping. More strategic consulting, like high-level strategic planning, business and financial management - things like that." I confirmed their understanding, "Yes I do." They inquired, "Well, we'd love for you to do that for us. We think we need it. Could you help us?" I explained, "Well, I could. But that would mean that I would be doing the work which is a much higher rate than a bookkeeper. They replied, "Okay, what's your hourly rate?" I said, "$192 an hour." They looked at each other, literally high-fived each other, and in unison said, "You're cheap!"

Frankly, no one had ever said that to me in response to hearing my hourly rate. Actually, most complained or gave a deep exhale when hearing my hourly rate. That was a funny moment. Then I added, "Yes, but I think what you're asking is probably going to be a 40 to 80-hour project, the strategic planning part." I continued, "I'll have to work it up, but I'm guessing based on what you've already said." They chimed, "That's fine. Once you work up a proposal, send it over to us."

Meeting over.

I sent the proposal over to them for about 80 hours of work at my hourly rate. They approved it and we moved forward. The initial strategic project was profitable - even though the other work was not profitable. That project led to more strategic work. About four or five months after the initial strategic engagement, I was doing anywhere from 10 to 15 hours a week myself at my rate for them. At the end of year one, they were one of my most profitable clients. And their firm had the most profitable year in its history due to the decisions we recommended and implemented for them. One thing I enjoyed about working with them is that they were brilliant and exceptional attorneys. They were great at what they did – even spoke multiple languages. One thing I learned about them is that they went to great law schools to be great at their profession, but not to be great at *running the business* of their profession. They did not like the "business" aspects of their professional very much at all.

That was how I began working with the law firm. It all started with me wanting to be obedient to what God said- as long as I liked and agreed with it! Once God told me something that was against what I believed was best for my business and against the foundations of how I ran my business, I did not want to do it. I confess to you that I did not want to obey what I heard. Eventually, I did obey. His path was a blessing to me and to our family. If I had stayed in my own thoughts and my own way of doing things, I would've never worked with them.

Sometimes following the Lord will challenge your own feelings and your own ways of thinking.

MY PRAYER FOR YOU:

I pray that you will allow the Lord to challenge your long-held beliefs or standards. I pray that you will be hopeful in following the Lord in the places He leads you. I pray you will trust that He has your best interest in mind in every moment of your life. I pray that you will see a small "ask" by a client, friend, or parent (lol) that could lead to blessings you never saw coming! I pray that when He asks you to do something which clearly pays no immediate profit, consider that He may have something in store for you down the road!

Bring Your Children to The Spirit of The Lord

This is a testimony you kids have probably heard about transitioning from one church that we attended shortly after I got saved. We attended this church since Stefen was a teenager, before you girls were born, and it was the only church home mom and I had known since coming to Christ. It is a fun testimony, really, because you kids all know JJ. JJ had been inviting us to a new church. We met him at the old church in the new believers' group at Dan and Lidia's house. We did life with JJ for many years before he moved to a "Spirit-filled" church.

JJ would invite us regularly to the new Spirit-filled church and I would say, "Nah, I'm not going to go. No, thanks. I'm happy where I am." Fast forward a bunch of years, and we started looking at changing churches.

At this point, we lived in Coppell and our church was in Dallas. You girls were getting into elementary school. We were trying to connect you with school relationships that were also church relationships because we watched Stefen struggle when he got to high school with those relationships being so separate. He had high school friends. He had church friends. They didn't mix or even know each other. I was really hoping that we would attend church where we lived, so you girls would have relationships in your school with kids that you also knew from church. That's where our hearts were leaning, so we started visiting some local churches.

We went ahead and visited one that was a Spirit-filled church that JJ attended about 15 minutes away. We liked it, but it was big for us and was not in our town. We had gone to the new members' class at the Spirit-filled church but didn't join. They also had Saturday services which we liked. We also visited a local church about 2 minutes away from our house. It seemed like half your elementary school went to this tiny little church. We visited those two churches while still attending our previous church. As we were going through that season, my friend JJ would invite us to his church often. You know JJ means well. And he loves us. And he's awesome. He would urge us, "I really think this is where you're supposed to be," (at his church). He would nag in a kind way, but it got annoying. I got to the point, where I demanded, "JJ, you need to shut up. Stop talking to me about it. If this is where I'm supposed to be, then God will tell me. I'm doing my best to hear the Lord and follow God. If this is where I'm supposed to be, he'll tell me." JJ stopped talking to me about coming to his church which was great! That gave me some peace, and some rest and took the pressure off.

One morning, right when I got to the office I heard the Lord say, "Clear your calendar. I want to spend the day with you." I replied, "Whoa, really? Okay." I told my assistant, "Hey there. I need your help! Please reschedule all the appointments I have today. I'm not going to be taking any calls. I will be in my office, but I'm going to spend the day with the Lord. I'll be reading, praying, and worshiping. And I don't want to be interrupted." She confirmed, "Okay, great." My calendar was cleared, and I spent the whole day, reading the Bible, praying, worshipping, and praising God! At about 2:30 pm in the afternoon, while I was face down on the floor worshipping, I heard, "Bring your children to where the Spirit of the Lord is, and they'll be fine." I knew exactly which church He meant. And I knew exactly why God told me that. He knew my heart was hurting and broken to see Stefen live through some of the challenges that he lived through. It was difficult for Stefen to be in a strongly secular high school with good friends. I mean, they're great friends around the neighborhood, but most of them weren't really led by the Lord. He had this separation in his life. He had church friends and he had school friends. It was hard. My heart ached for him and knew that was a difficult season of life for him. I didn't want you girls to live with the same struggle. God knew that concern had been on my heart for a while and was something I deeply cared about. After I heard what God said, I called mom and inquired, "can we talk tonight after the kids go to bed?" "Sure," she chirped.

But here's the REALLY cool part.

At four o'clock in the afternoon, JJ calls me, "Hey, how you doing?" I smiled, "I'm good." He stammers, "Hey, so ... " He was stammering and beating around the bush. Finally, he blurts out, "So listen. Early this morning at five am in my quiet time, the Lord shared this with me. So this isn't me. This is the Lord. And I want you to know that I have not wanted to tell you. He told me he wanted me to call you and tell you this. And I have not wanted to do it all day long. I've been avoiding it. Finally, the Lord convicted me and said, "Are you going to call him or what?" Do you know what JJ said? JJ said that God told him to call me and tell me, "Take your children to where the Spirit of the Lord is, and they'll be fine!"

It was verbatim what I heard at 2:30 pm in the afternoon. When JJ told me, I started laughing. He wondered, "You're not mad at me?" I chimed in, "Nope, I'm not mad at you." He continued, "Why are you laughing?" I announced, "Welllllll, I have something to tell you." I told him what happened that morning in clearing my calendar, and that the Lord had already told me at 2:30 pm what he just told me! JJ started cheering on the phone. He was so excited. Then he asked excitedly, "Have you told Jennifer?" "No, not yet. I set an appointment with her to talk to her about it tonight," I replied. JJ exclaimed, "Wow. Praise the Lord. That is so cool."

That is how we were told and confirmed that we needed to take y'all to the new church which we still attend to this day 15 years later! I thought that was a super cool, fun testimony about hearing God and letting him be the Lord of all those decisions. I love y'all and it's so much fun to share the testimony with you.

MY PRAYER FOR YOU

I pray that you will understand that the Bible is full of people walking and talking with the Lord and that in His Holy Spirit is where He wants us to be! I pray you will realize that God already knows the deepest longings and desires of your heart – and that He wants to meet those in His way. I pray that there is NOTHING that can separate you from His love and grace. I pray for boldness in each of you to follow Him even if you have to reschedule appointments, meetings, or classes.

Where Your Girls Will Go

S o this is a really fun God moment testimony to share with y'all. It's
when we transitioned you girls out of public school over to Faith
Christian School.

It began with some challenges we were having at the elementary
school with some girls bullying and being mean-spirited to y'all. We
approached the public school to talk to them. I asked the teacher,
"Could you schedule an appointment with the other kid and their
parents so we can talk this out together and help the kids come to
a place of unity and reconciliation to move past this?" The teacher
stated, "Actually, no. I can't do that. That would be against our school
district privacy policy." I was stunned, "What? What are you talking
about?" I continued, "My son went through this school district. And
graduated from the high school in this school district. Trust me. We
had quite a few appointments with other kids and their parents. It
was very helpful and very productive getting everybody in the same
room." She cautioned, "Well, that has changed. We are no longer able
to schedule any appointments like that. Matter of fact, I'm not even
allowed to talk to you about this other kid. I can only talk to you about

your kid." I was stunned, "Yeah, but this other kid is impacting my kid by bullying and picking on her." I declared, "This isn't going well. We need to have a meeting. Whether I do it with the principal or whatever, but this isn't right." The teacher gently shared, "I appreciate your thoughts. But I can't do that. It would be a violation of our privacy policy." I contended, "How are we ever going to teach kids to work things out if we can't have a meeting and discuss it?" The teacher was really kind. She gently replied, "Off the record, I totally agree with you. On the record, this is the privacy policy, and we can't do that. I cannot facilitate that meeting."

I remember going home, talking to Mom, and thinking, "this is so strange". After that, I wanted to get out of that school district and away from the type of leadership where we cannot address things that are going on at the school. What am I supposed to do? File an assault charge against this little kid? How do you reconcile? How do you work things out? What is the policy? If we can't ever address things, then things will never get better. It was really, really mind-blowing that the school district had implemented that policy.

Nonetheless, we started praying about what to do school-wise. We thought about moving farther out to a smaller town. We had already been thinking about high school, even though you girls were only at the beginning of elementary. Then we started considering a Christian school, a little private school, or something like that. We really weren't sure.

Then one Sunday night, I'm watching a Sunday Sports TV show here in the Dallas area. They did an expose on a high school football game that was between a Christian school and these kids who were inmates at a juvie prison in North Texas. They showed highlights of the game. They showed the breakthrough. They showed all this kind of stuff. Then they were interviewing the inmate kids after the game. They're all felons, but they're still high school kids. And they're interviewing these kids on TV. I've told y'all before that I got in lots of trouble as a kid, so I do have a heart for at-risk youth and kids that get in trouble. I just don't feel like getting in trouble as a kid needs to be the verdict on their whole life.

The broadcasters were interviewing these kids.

They were criminals, and they were crying! And talking about how this gives them hope when they get out. You see, the parents of this Christian school made a breakthrough for the prison football team to run through when the game started. Those kids never ran through a breakthrough at any of their games because ALL of their games were AWAY games! The parents also printed out a roster of the first names of the prisoner team and were cheering for them by name on the Visitor side of the field. One of the kids confessed through tears, "this gives me hope for when I get out that maybe not everyone's going to judge me." I was moved to tears. Here I am, watching the Sports Special in the living room at 10:30/11:00 at night on a Sunday. Everybody's in bed and I'm bawling on the living room floor, and thinking, "wow, what an amazing thing this school did".

The athletic director, or maybe the coach, comes on and they interview him. He said, "Well, I didn't do all this. All I did was send an email out asking if a few parents would be willing to sit on the other side, the visitor's section because none of the students' parents are allowed to know where they're playing or where they're going to be for security reasons. So this team never has anyone on their sidelines cheering for them." He asked if a few parents would do that. That night, the Christian school parents rallied and ALL of them sat on the juvi prison side of the stadium! The prison football team sideline was full of people cheering for them. It was really, really cool.

While I'm sitting there on my knees watching and crying, I heard the Lord say, "This is your school. This is where your girls will go". I thought, "Oh my gosh. This is great." I didn't even know where it was located. I'd never heard of that school. I had to go find the school. Turns out it was in Grapevine, which is right around the corner from Coppell. I thought, "wow, how cool".

We began the process of having you guys do the assessments and testing. The Lord told me you're both going to go to school next semester in the Fall. But after we did the assessments and whatnot, they let us know that they only had a spot for Gracemarie, which was a 4th-grade spot. They said would not have a spot for you, Jillienne, until the spring. Basically, they were full. But the Lord had already told me she was going to start the Fall semester. It's going to happen. I remember Mom asking me, "Hey since she's not going to start right away, do you want me to wait on buying a uniform?" And I confirmed, "Don't wait. Go ahead and get a uniform. She's going to start. She's going to start this semester. That's what I heard." And Mom retorted, "Well, the admissions person told me there's no spot available for her." I reassured mom, "I know that that's what she said. I'm telling you what God told me. Please get her a uniform, and get her all ready to go. It's going to happen."

I kid you not, Jillienne! You started school on a Thursday or a Friday at the public school. And somewhere in that timeframe, we found out that a spot did open up for you in 2nd grade. You started on Monday or Tuesday the next week at Grapevine Faith. That is how we made the transition from public school to Faith. Started out tough but ended awesomely! We already had your uniform ready and you were good to go. I know Jillienne, you weren't too happy about it because you were really happy with your homeroom teacher at the public school. I know neither one of you was super excited about it, but these were decisions we made being led by the Lord and letting him be in charge of our lives.

I wanted to share this testimony with you because I know it had some heartache at the time. I understand that it's hard to leave the friends you had at public school. We believe this is what God wanted us to do and how the Lord led us to this decision. I love you~

MY PRAYER FOR YOU:

I pray that you will forgive us for the heartache you experienced when you changed schools. I pray that you will trust that we were just doing our best to follow God's will for you. I pray you will know that God said you would go to that school. I pray that you will see that you were surrounded by children whose *parents* would go out of their way to love the broken, downcast, and criminal. I pray you would trust that we were excited for you to be around kids who had parents like that!

You're Moving

On a Sunday night in March during my alone time with God, the Holy Spirit told me, "Get your finances together. You're moving." I was excited, "OK cool!" I immediately went to tell Mom what I heard. She countered, "We are in a lease until August and it's March. God would not have us break a contract. That would not be right." I responded, "I understand, but it's what He told me and I think we need to do it. He said to get finances together and that we are moving- He didn't say when." Mom agreed and we trusted God would do something about our lease if it came to that. So the next day, I called JJ and told him what the Lord said to me Sunday night. I know y'all know JJ is a good friend and a faithful spirit-filled believer and he's also a realtor. JJ immediately began searching for homes for us and sent them to me. I noticed that he sent 5-bedroom homes to me. Our home on Creekside was only three bedrooms. One for mom and me. One for you girls. And we had an empty bedroom since Stefen had moved out. In my mind, I didn't need five bedrooms. I needed two! Three max. So I told JJ what I felt we needed. JJ retorted, "Have you asked God?" I said, "No. I don't need to ask God about wasting my money and getting more house than I need. Please send me three-bedroom houses." JJ replied, "I think you need to ask God!" Well, I didn't. And JJ kept sending me 5-bedroom homes that whole week!

Then Friday of that same week I got an email from our land-lord. The subject line read: Selling 123 Creekside Lane (This was our address!!)

Wow…. God knew. I immediately remembered that JESUS promised that the Holy Spirit would come when He leaves "who would tell us of things to come." Wow.

An email that could have easily gotten us all tense and anxious about having to move was COMPLETELY turned around by God. We were already preparing to move. Ha! SO COOL! When I shared that with our landlord, he was stoked for us. He had not had experiences like that with the Lord yet and wanted to talk more about that. His email let us know that they were going to sell and wanted us to have time to choose another home to lease. And if we wanted to buy the home, he wanted us to have the first choice. And if we found something before August, he would just end the lease. Win-Win. No penalties or extra charges. Wow!

So that weekend, we looked at homes. Nothing seemed to gel. Looked again on Monday, but nothing. I was getting frustrated and to make matters worse, JJ kept sending me five-bedroom houses. I told him Monday afternoon, "don't send me another 5-bedroom house." He said, "I keep hearing 5-bedroom when I ask the Lord "what do You want me to show them?"." I contended, "We don't need 5 bedrooms and I'm not gonna be a poor steward again! I've gone down that road and I'm not doing it again!!!"

I was frustrated before going to bed that night.

In the middle of the night that Monday night, I woke up. When I woke up, I asked God, "did you wake me up, Lord?" I heard, "Yes. Get up. I'm going to show you your home." Excited, I jumped out of bed and headed to the living room. As I walked into the living room,

I heard, "Where are you going?" I replied, "To my laptop. To login to realtor.com. I thought that's what you meant when you were gonna show me my house". God replied, "get your bible. Turn to psalms." As I got my bible and started to turn to Psalms, I asked, "what number?" "23", He whispered. As I began to read, I realized it was the well-known 23rd Psalm. I read.

1 The Lord is my shepherd, I lack nothing. **2** He makes me lie down in green pastures, he leads me beside quiet waters, **3** he refreshes my soul. He guides me along the right paths for his name's sake. **4** Even though I walk through the darkest valley, I will fear no evil, for you are with me; your rod and your staff, they comfort me. **5** You prepare a table before me in the presence of my enemies. You anoint my head with oil; my cup overflows. **6** Surely your goodness and love will follow me all the days of my life, and I will dwell in the house of the Lord forever.

The moment I read that last verse, I heard "you will dwell in my house all your days." Complete peace came over me. I had a sense that no matter where I lived, I lived in HIS HOUSE. "Yes," I declared. "I understand. Thank you, Father." "Is this it? Can I go back to bed now?" "Yes," I heard.

I crawled back into bed. As I lay there, I asked God "Is there anything you wanna tell me before I go back to sleep?" I heard, "Yes. Your home will be ready in the morning." I laughed and said, "How am I supposed to sleep now???!!!! Lol…" and fell back to sleep laughing.

In the morning, I told Mom what happened the night before. She was excited. We prayed and asked the Holy Spirit where to look. Mom heard "It's in your backyard". We both interpreted that to mean Grapevine. We lived in Coppell at the time and Grapevine was the town next to us. We drive y'all to school in Grapevine and we go through Grapevine every weekend on our way to worship. So we headed to Grapevine and drove around different neighborhoods. After a bit of this, we stopped and prayed for guidance again. I saw a vision of trees. We heard, "You will know it when you see it." We ventured again through the wooded and winding roads of Grapevine taking turn after turn, asking the Lord where and when to turn, all the while allowing Him to lead us. Until… the last turn.

As we turned a narrow winding corner which seemed more like someone's driveway than a shady country road, we saw a sign in a yard. I slowed. Mom and I looked at each other. That was it. We knew it when we saw it! I turned into the driveway. Just then, a construction truck pulled up at the curb and the man inside walked up to the front door. He saw us in our car in the driveway and said "Y'all wanna come inside and take a look?" We agreed and hopped out of our car asap! As we walked through the home, we were more and more excited. Mom actually did a herkey jump! I think the construction guy thought she was crazy!!!

Guess how many bedrooms it had? FIVE!!!

Each of you girls was able to get your own room. We had our room. But what about the other two? It was a couple of months later when we learned the reason we needed five bedrooms. Stefen called and needed a place for himself and his daughter Hayden to live since he was having marriage challenges. Of course! We had two bedrooms for y'all! I wept with gratitude when I got off the phone with Stefen.

God knew.

As a result of this experience, I have learned to ask God. Even when I feel, believe, and think I know what would be wise and according to His scripture. His ways are higher than my ways. He knows what I need. Those who are led by the Spirit.

MY PRAYER FOR YOU:

I pray that you would know the excitement, joy, and adventure of being led by the Spirit of the Living God! I pray that you will let Him lead you in the important, the mundane, and especially the ones where you think "I've already screwed up like that, so I'm not gonna do that again." I pray you will forgive us for decisions that caused you pain that we didn't explain very well at the time.

He Will Receive You

It was Christmas Day 2011. All of my siblings and their families were gathered at my house for Christmas. Late in the afternoon, my oldest brother began to quietly ask my siblings and me to meet him in another room away from the kids. All of us quietly slipped away to another room where he proceeded to share that he received a call from my Dad, or maybe the hospital where he was located, which reported that my dad was going to hospice care and had about a day or so to live.

My dad lived about 4-5 hours away in the hill country of Texas. Prior to that Christmas Day, the last time I had a conversation with my dad was about five years earlier. Although, I did call him in October 2011 when I was told he would only live a few days. When I called the hospital that October, he answered in his room, but did not say anything. I said, "Dad, it's Mark." Silence. "Dad, you there?" Silence. "Well, if you can hear me, I love you." Silence. I hung up.

A little back history about not talking to my dad- some of it y'all know, some of it, you don't know. Five years earlier during Christmas break when we were visiting PeePaw, he kept disrespecting me. He would cuss in front of y'all after I asked him not to. He also attempted to override my instructions to y'all kids saying that it's "his house" versus the plain fact that I'm your dad! The final issue for me was what he did after I had come out from a nap to ask y'all to quiet down while I was trying to sleep. The moment I got back to my room to sleep, I heard the stereo turned WAAAAAY up. I knew my dad did that because none of y'all would disrespect me like that. I sat there thinking, "I'm 40 years old and he still treats me like I'm some little kid. I don't have to put up with this any longer. It's not healthy for me." So I packed all our luggage from our room and put it in the suburban. I quietly and respectfully went out to the Christmas tree and bagged up all y'all's presents. Then I quietly let each of you know that it was time to go. We left quietly and without a fight or issue. We left on December 26, although we had planned to stay the whole week. Apparently, the next day PeePaw emailed and called Mom encouraging her to divorce me! Mom didn't tell me at first because she thought he was upset, and it would go away. He proceeded to contact her for months. He offered to pay for a place for mom and y'all to stay encouraging her to divorce me. What the???! Mom finally told me after a few months of emails. Needless to say, I called him and said he crossed the line by attempting to come between what God has put together. And if he wasn't my father I'd be at his door telling him this face to face! I told him that until he apologized, we wouldn't be having any contact with him. Not me. Not Jen. Not my kids. Until he apologized! If he's man enough to try to break us up, then he can be man enough to apologize. He never apologized. Even worse, he accelerated the remaining amount of a business loan I had with him, sent a demand letter for the full amount, and then sued me - knowing full well that I was unable to pay the large sum all at once with Stefen in college and with my money tied up in my business. The court process took months until a final court date was set in late November. The final amount he sued me for including attorney costs was about 24k.

Cool testimony on this though! SOOO, my "bruthaman" Mike G from college had been living out of state for a while. He and I had planned months earlier to connect when he got in town over Thanksgiving break. Turns out, the court date with my dad was a few days after that. Since Mike and I hadn't talked in a long time, we decided to meet up for lunch early Thanksgiving week. We had a long lunch catching up and sharing about life. In the past, I was prideful when it came to money. I especially did not want anyone to know if I was having money challenges. But I felt that I needed to be open and honest with Mike. So I shared the stress of the court situation and how it might end up as a judgment against me and would not be a good thing for my professional career. Mike immediately said, "I wanna take care of that for you." I protested, "What? No way. I can't let you do that." Mike said, "No, you listen to me. Right before I got on the plane to fly here, I had some options come into the money that I was not expecting. It's sitting in my account right now. On the plane, I was asking God what does He want me to do with it? Well, this is it. This is what I'm supposed to do with the money!" I started crying right there in the restaurant. God delivered the answer in a most surprising way from a friend who was following God! Another SUPER COOL thing was that the amount of the money Mike received was within a couple of hundred dollars of what the court was requesting. Hallelujah!!!

Yes, it was horrible for my dad/PeePaw to try to ruin my marriage and our family, and then put such a financial strain on all of us. Regardless, I forgave him but kept a healthy boundary in place for the next five years.

So here I was on Christmas Day hearing that my father had about one day to live. Some blood number was below 10 and it's supposed to be much higher. The doctor had never known anyone below 10 because most people die before that number is reached. My father's death was imminent. I recall that a couple of my brothers decided to leave that night to see him. Everyone knew that PeePaw and I weren't talking, so no one anticipated I would go. And quite frankly, I wasn't sure if I would or not. I decided I would ask God about it first.

The next morning in my alone time with God, I was telling God about all the pain, betrayal, and rejection I had endured at the hand of my dad. My dad also had crazy violent moments when I was a kid. I got past that and attempted to have a relationship with him as an adult- then his efforts to ruin my marriage, family, and career happened. I couldn't drive down and endure another rejection. I told God, "I don't wanna get rejected again." I heard God say, "He will receive you." I said, "Really?" "Yes." I then asked if he wanted me to take my son Stefen (my dad had always been so good to Stefen). Another "Yes." I went out to find Mom and let her know what the Lord had told me. She hugged me. Mom knew how painful it had been waiting five years for an apology.

Stefen and I left that morning to see PeePaw.

When we arrived at the hospital and found his room, we walked in quietly. My brothers looked shocked to see me. I looked at my dad in his hospital bed with all his cables and oxygen tubes attached to him. He must have heard the door open because he looked toward me. Then he reached out his hand to receive me! I took his hand. We rested at that moment for a while. It was just as God said it would be! He received me. Later that day, he was transported home for the remainder of hospice. What followed was such a holy, precious, and intimate week of hospice care at his home with all my siblings and the oldest two grandsons. He passed on January 2, 2012. Eight days later instead of one!

Praise God!

MY PRAYER FOR YOU:

I pray that you will forgive PeePaw and me for our flaws and the time lost with him. I pray you know that PeePaw loved each of you dearly. I pray you will know that PeePaw pointed me to Jesus my whole life by taking my family to church each Sunday morning at 8 am. I pray you will know that reconciliation is part of God's plan. I pray you will trust God when He gives you guidance, even when you have apprehension.

Your Faith Has Healed You

This is one of my super favorite God moments to share with you. Gosh, this was a very long time ago, somewhere in, I think 2008 timeframe. This testimony is about Grammy and healing.

At one of the businesses I owned, I would stay late on Wednesday nights to do a lot of financial planning and administrative work for my clients. Grammy would come and I'd pay her to help. She was a great help to me because she had her insurance and securities licenses at one point. She would come every other Wednesday night. One summer night while we were working, Grammy shared a little bit about her liver in the beginning stages of cirrhosis. After she tells me all about the illness and the ailments, I asked Grammy, "Hey, do you believe that God can heal you?" Grammy hemmed and hawed for a second, "Well, I suppose he could. I just don't know that he would." I said, "Okay." We had only been attending the church we were at for a year or so but I knew that they had a healing ministry. I shared that with Grammy, "Well, I know my church has a healing ministry and I've heard of quite a few people who have been healed." (And at the time we were members and I wasn't on staff.) Grammy replied, "Okay, well, that's interesting." She continued, "Do you know when they have it?" "I really don't. I don't really know any of the details. I just know that they have it. I thought I'd let you know," I replied. And Grammy chimed, "Okay, cool. Thank you very much." That was the end of that, or so I thought.

Two weeks later, she comes up to work on a Wednesday night and she starts, "Hey, didn't you tell me that you guys go to your church on Saturday evening?" I said, "Yeah." She questioned, "Well, which service do you go to?" I replied, "Well, we go to the 4:00." She exclaimed, "Great." She then firmly inquired, "What do you think about me coming with you to the 4:00 service, this coming weekend? Then after that, go with me over to this healing center? The healing center that they have at your church is at a different building and we'd have to drive over there but it's not very far away and it closes at 6:00. And so I'm wondering, would that work for you if I went to church with y'all and then you would go with me over to the healing center and I could have someone pray for healing for me?"

I got a big ole smile on my face and laughed. Grammy had planned out the whole thing. And I confirmed, "Absolutely. I'll be happy to do that." I offered, "Mom, do you know that there are places in scripture where Jesus literally tells a woman, 'Woman, your faith has healed you?'" Grammy replied, "Oh, I might have heard of that. Yeah, I think so." I said, "I don't know Mom. I'm sitting here thinking. Look at all that you've planned out. Look what you've researched. You found out all of this and now I have this strange feeling that your faith is going to heal you. You're going to get healed!" Grammy smiled and came back with, "Well, I certainly hope so."

That's not the end of the testimony!

Saturday rolls around and Grammy goes with us to service. We're sitting in service and our friend JJ is sitting on the other side of Grammy. Grammy knew JJ so they were talking before the service began. We're also chatting and meeting people and talking with folks. The service always began with worship, then a message and prayer time afterward. During the first worship song, the Lord told JJ to give Grammy his bookmark. JJ had a bookmark from the Freedom ministry which he loved. JJ said that was the most favorite bookmark he ever owned. JJ was very torn when the Lord gave him that instruction, but he turned to Grammy right after the worship song and said, "The Lord told me to give this to you."

After the worship songs, right when we started sitting down, the pastor encouraged, "Hey, greet people around you. Say hello!" Grammy turns to me, "Did you tell them that I'm coming for healing?" I retorted, "What are you talking about?" Grammy continues, "Well, all the worship songs were about healing. Did you tell them?" And I said, "No. I'm nobody at this church. There are thousands of people that go to this church and I don't know anyone like that. That's not necessarily how they would make a decision on how to choose a worship song anyhow~ based on one person making a song request, so to speak." We both chuckled about that. But Grammy was really excited that the songs were about healing.

After service, we were sitting around talking with one of the ladies in front of us named Wendy. Grammy's right there, so I introduced the two of them. I introduced Grammy to our friend as Kathryn because Grammy goes by Kathryn to people who don't know her. But for the people that do know her, she goes by Kathy. The introduction was short and sweet. Then Grammy started talking to JJ. We continued talking with Wendy.

Wendy then asked, "Hey, does your mom go by the name of Kathy?" I replied, "Actually, she does to people who know her, but she doesn't introduce herself like that. If you don't know her, she always says Kathryn." Wendy replied, "Oh my God." Her eyes got all big. She exclaimed, "Oh my gosh, I think this is her." And I said, "What do you mean?" She shared, "Well, about six months ago in my prayer time, the Lord said to me, 'I want you to start praying for healing for Kathy,' and so I have been. I pray every day for healing for Kathy. And every time someone has a prayer request for healing or health for a woman, I always ask, 'Is your sister or mother or aunt,' whomever the woman is, I always ask them, 'Does she go by Kathy?' And you're the first person to say, 'Yes.' So I think I've been praying for your mom's healing."

I started laughing and said, "Well, guess what? Do you know why she's here? She came here because this is a 4:00 service. We are literally leaving here in a second to go over to the healing rooms for her to be prayed over for healing." Wendy was so excited, "Oh my gosh, it's her, it's her. Do you mind if I tell her?" I encouraged her, "Please do! I think this'll be great." I turned to Grammy, "Hey, Mom, my friend Wendy has something she wants to tell you!" Wendy went on to share with Grammy everything God had instructed her. Grammy's eyes were like saucers. She was like, "Oh my gosh. This is pretty amazing!" Then we prayed together and thanked Wendy for her encouragement. So that happened, and we hadn't even gotten to the Healing Center yet!

What I didn't know at the time, but I found out later, is that Grammy had gone to the doctor six months earlier and received the cirrhosis of the liver early detection then! And a few days after this healing room visit, Grammy was going back for her six-month checkup. The doctor gave Grammy a list of things to do or change in her life and to come back in six months. Well, Grammy either didn't do all of them or she didn't do any of them! Grammy knew she was about to go back in for her checkup this following week. And our friend Wendy had been praying for six months for Kathy, who happens to be our Grammy!

When we go to the Healing Center, the prayer team invites all of us in to pray with them. We (mom, Gracemarie, Jillienne, and I) all went in with the people to lay hands and pray over Grammy for healing. We prayed over her and that was it. Grammy's follow-up doctor's appointment was the next Tuesday. Tuesday came and went. I did not hear from Grammy. When I reached out to Grammy, she said something happened to the test and somehow they were compromised (I don't remember the medical term for it). The doctor's office scheduled her to come in to redo the test on Thursday.

On Thursday, Grammy called me and excitedly questioned, "Hey, are you sitting down?" I said, "No, but I feel pretty confident about what you're about to tell me!" Exuberantly, she blurted out, "You're never going to believe it. All my levels were normal. I'm no longer even close to having cirrhosis of the liver!" We were cheering "Woo, woo!" On top of that, Grammy added, "Hey, ever since Saturday, I have not used my CPAP machine!" I didn't even know she was using a CPAP machine. I quipped, "What are you talking about?" Grammy shared, "Well, I fell asleep that night without my CPAP on. I've been able to breathe and sleep wonderfully ever since Saturday night. So not only is my liver fine, but I'm sleeping fine and no longer have to use that machine!"

Is that cool or what?

Watching Grammy step out in faith and research where the healing rooms were located (which I had never been to before at our church), and seeing all that God did in Grammy is so powerful to me. I'm so grateful to God to see Him move in her and encourage her faith!

I love you~

MY PRAYER FOR YOU:

I pray you know that God heals. I pray that you will realize that YOUR FAITH is integral to healing and following God. I pray that when you get an "assignment" to pray for a name or person, or face God gives you, you will be faithful to honor God as He trusted you enough to give it to you! I pray you recognize that God can, is, and will direct your steps as you exercise faith.

Those Three

I want to share this next testimony with you because it was a big surprise to me when it happened and really stood out in my own life. I don't know if y'all remember when I was doing juvie prison ministry. I would lead a team to go in once a month and do a worship service, then pray for and visit with the young men in the prison. Juvie prison ministry has been near and dear to my heart since I got into lots of trouble with the law as a kid. I think there's so much more life available to kids who are in prison. I believe that most juvie inmates just acted out of the environment that they found themselves in.

One Saturday afternoon, I was finalizing the lesson to preach the next day. I remember thanking God for keeping me from killing anyone back when I used to run around and get in trouble. I had a .22 and a .38 I carried when I was drug dealing and committing crimes. I thanked God, "Thank you God so much that I didn't kill anyone back in the day when I was getting in trouble." Ever so quietly but firmly, I heard, "What about those three?" Instantly, I knew what God meant. I immediately thought of the three abortions that I was a part of and had a role in. I wept in acknowledgment of the grace and kindness God showed me at that moment. And for the gentleness in how He revealed me to me! I did participate in those abortions. I had a hand in that. His love and grace wrecked me at that moment. No condemnation. No judgment. Just a kind word of awareness. I was undone, just weeping.

And here I was trying to prepare a message to preach.

All the kids at the prison were felons. They all committed serious crimes, but none were convicted of killing anyone. What the Lord said to me seemed relevant to share with them. I shared that whole story with them, and how God brought the truth to me just as I was preparing the lesson. I shared the graciousness God had towards me and the kindness he had towards me. I knew there was no guilt, no shame, no condemnation when I heard him say, "what about those three?" When I thought of the abortions, I was not guilt-ridden. When He asked the question, I felt His grace, His mercy, and the completeness of which He has saved me - all my sins, every single one. There's nothing, there's just nothing that He hasn't already paid for.

That was the message for me. For the young men in prison. For all of us.

I wanted to share that with y'all. You'll probably have a sin or two in your life that you think, oh my gosh, I can't believe I did that; or that's horrible or horrific, or there's no way God can love me after this. Those types of moments happen. I just wanted to encourage you that God absolutely loves you. He has already sent Jesus for you. Jesus is already sacrificed. He is the sacrificial lamb that atones for all of our sins. I just wanted to share that with you. Obviously, I'm not proud of participating in three abortions. I wish that those things had not happened. Yet I know God's mercy knows no end. He literally remembers my sin no more. The Bible says my sins are as far as the east is from the west. I just wanted to encourage you and let y'all know I love you. That moment just kind of rocked me, but also gave me a fullness of, and confidence of, knowing just the completeness of God's love, His mercy, and His forgiveness.

MY PRAYER FOR YOU:

I pray that you will recognize that Jesus has paid the FULL price for your sin. I pray you will not run away from God when you do something you think is BIG. I pray you will know that His love and mercies are endless and more than enough to atone for your sin. I pray you will each learn that there is no condemnation, no judgment, and no guilt for those who are in Christ!

When I Release You

Hey, y'all. I want to share with you how the Lord led me into biblical counseling and how He led me into what I'm doing with my life. It really began at our local church worship service. One day, they announced that a Christian university was going to be moving from Los Angeles to our local church in Southlake, Texas. It would come under the oversight of our local church, and they would be offering university classes right here. Man, the moment they brought that up, my heart leaped. Something inside of me was like, "Awesome. Yes!"

The church and university had some interest meetings in the evenings. One Wednesday night, they were having a Q&A session to learn about the school. If you turned in your application that night, the application fee would be waived. I was pretty sure I was going to enroll in classes but had not decided on a program – which was required to turn in an application. The two master's programs that have always interested me are counseling and messianic studies. I really love the history of the Bible and the Jewish people, yet for most of my career, I've advised or counseled people in one area or another related to business, finances, investments, or even personal matters in life groups. I had to choose before I turned in the application that night, so I was praying about it that day. When it was time to leave, I didn't have the app completed yet. I didn't want to be late, so I said to myself as I got in the car, "You know, I guess I'll figure it out."

Like most meetings at our local church, we begin with worship. While I'm worshiping, I heard, "Worship." I thought, "What?" I mean. I'm literally singing, hands up, standing up, and I heard in my thoughts, "Worship," and I was like, "Okaaaay." Even though I was still singing with my voice, in my mind I was having this conversation. I said to God, "Okay. What does that mean?" He said, "I love it when you worship Me. Worship. I want you to study worship." "Whoa," was the first thing I thought! My thoughts began to race, "Oh my gosh. That is not even on my radar." "Oh my gosh." I was so shocked. I heard it again, "Worship. I love it when you worship Me." I finally said, "Okay."

I filled out my application. Turned it in for worship. Began my master's program in the Fall under the worship program. You know, it was pretty hard because, number one, it wasn't my jam. You know what I mean? I mean, I loved to worship. Don't get me wrong. The coursework was related to obviously studying worship, as well as musically-oriented praise and singing. Number two, I was the oldest guy in every single class. Everybody else is young and most lead worship at their local church. The kids were wearing all these skinny jeans and cool hair. I mean, the average age of students was probably like 20. Some classes were hybrid undergrad/graduate classes where the in-class content was the same, but the out-of-class work was different. I had even 18-year-olds in the class working on their undergrad whereas I'm in my mid-40s working on my master's. Lastly, I knew that this was something that I wasn't that great at, but I absolutely knew that God told me, "Worship." Pretty much everybody I know said something like, "Are you sure?" Then people would ask me, "Do you play an instrument? I mean, can you sing?" Most people thought worship was basically about upfront leading worship at a church service. I kinda thought that too. And it is one aspect of worship. But it's not the only aspect of worship that you'll find in the Bible.

Every time I had to write a paper in this program, I would tell God, "Oh my gosh, God, I absolutely need Your help. I feel so inadequate. I don't know exactly what the teacher's looking for and I'm not quite sure what to write. I got nothing. I absolutely need Your help. Please help me write this paper." It was a pretty tough seven months of classes. But it was cool because it led me to a really cool place with the Lord. One day in the spring of 2013, I was sitting up at campus working on a paper and before I started the paper, I told the Lord again, "You know what, Lord, I got nothing. I really need Your help. Help me write this one too. You've already helped me so many times. Please help me write this paper." I heard Him say, "When I release you into your strengths, I want you to have this same posture." I inquired, "What?" He said, "When I release you into your strengths, I want you to have this same posture." I pursued, "You mean like "I got nothing?" I heard, "Yes. Yes, definitely." I responded, "Oh my gosh, so are You saying I don't have to keep studying worship anymore???" He said, "Yeah. I'm releasing you, but I want you to have this same posture when I release you into your strengths." I cheered, "Woop!! Hallelujah!!!" I was ready to get out of worship. God took me through these seven months of classes where I couldn't rely on myself and what I already knew. Does that make sense? I needed Him to help me get through those classes. He trained me to lean on Him and to trust Him. I was not able to rely on myself like I typically did in other areas of my life. Trusting Him was the lesson!

This was a really cool lesson because some people thought, or were concerned, that what I heard from the Lord wasn't from the Lord. Or that I made it up. Or what am I doing with worship? It would be easy to have doubts while in the program, but I knew that I knew that

I knew that He said "worship". I didn't know the reason at the time. It didn't make sense. It was illogical. It didn't resonate necessarily with me. Me? Worship? I mean, I knew when I heard Him, it was God. Even though I didn't "get it", I went and did it. I was obedient.

Maybe that's the best thing I could share with you. When you know that you know it is God, then obey Him.

"Have the same posture" ~ a posture of reliance on Him. It was a lesson for me as I moved into His giftings, abilities, and strengths which He wired into me. I typically would be very self-reliant when in my comfort zone and strengths. However, each time I have a session, I pray and inquire of the Lord before someone comes in. I rely on God. I'm talking to the Lord while I'm in the session. Even if I have a sense of what I think is going on, I still submit myself to the Lord. It's like, "Hey, I need You. Lead me, guide me. Cuz I got nothing."

MY PRAYER FOR YOU:

I pray you will be willing to follow God even when things don't make sense. Yet, I will encourage you to ensure what you "hear" from the Lord does not contradict His Holy Word in the Bible. I pray you will pursue His will in all your decisions. I pray you will trust that He has your long-term blessing and goodness in mind as He leads you!

You're Going to
Be a Shepherd

My transition into vocational ministry was another God moment-this time, it changed the trajectory and focus of my life (and y'alls life too when I think about it)!

The God moment really began a few months earlier in my alone time with the Lord. He told me that I was going to be transitioning from the law firm where I worked. I had planned a weekend sabbatical to gain focus on my next role. As the sabbatical weekend approached, I received an email invitation to a one-day Connect event featuring Robert Morris and Jimmy Evans. When I receive the invite, I heard "Go". I clarified with the Lord- "Really? You want me to go to this? But that is the first day of my sabbatical with YOU!! I want to spend that day with YOU!" He said, "Go".

I went.

The event ended at about 3p, and I began my sabbatical immediately afterward at the lake. I parked in an isolated place at the lake where I like to go. I opened my car door, rolled down the windows, put on worship music, and closed my eyes to worship. After worshipping for a while, I began to ask God about my future and my next role. He stated, "I'm taking you through a new season where you will have to humble yourself more than you ever have before." I was a bit apprehensive when I heard that because I wasn't humble at all. I had accomplished many things in my life, risen to leadership roles, was very well compensated, and did that mostly on my own – so I thought. I inquired, "What do you mean by humble?" I heard "Become low". I questioned, "How low?"

I immediately had a vision.

In the vision, I was high up in the sky, about 20,000 feet, soaring as if on the wings of an eagle on a bright sunny day. I could see beautiful mountains, valleys, and canyons below me which looked etched into the land by the fingers of God. Since I had visited Colorado quite a bit, been to the Grand Canyon, and skydived a couple of times, I loved the scenery in the vision! I was descending in a broad circular pattern towards the canyon. Slowly circling and getting closer to the ground. It was surreal and lovely at the same time~ and super quiet like the descent of a skydiver after the chute has opened. Then we reached the ground level at the edge of the canyon but kept going lower and lower into the canyon. I descended even lower to where the sunlight became dim. As I floated lower, I gently landed on the sandy loam at the very, very bottom of the canyon- below ground level. While face down in the sandy loam, I heard "This low".

I lamented, "Dang, that's low." But the vision was so beautiful and cool! It included so many things I've enjoyed in my life- skydiving, mountain climbing/hiking, and rafting through canyons! I thanked God for the vision, and acknowledged "Ok, I need to humble myself." But as I thought about it, the vision didn't really give me concrete, actionable intel on how to get low. Or how to humble myself. So I said to the Lord- "the vision was great! So cool! But how do I *ACTUALLY* humble myself?" "Stop taking credit for things," He declared. "You've been taking credit for things your whole life that was me!" He gently continued, "You raised your son by yourself? No, I was with you! You put yourself through college? No, I provided for you! You started successful businesses? No, I lead you. Who do you think gave you those great business ideas? I gave you your ideas! I gave you your tenacity! I gave you your perseverance! I gave you your personality! I gave you your intellect! All that you have and all that you are came from me!" His words cascaded over me gently, yet firmly.

I was undone. I was literally sobbing at the edge of the lake. God was right. I would say all those things about myself. I did not acknowledge God at all in those areas of my life. I took credit for so many things in my life.

While the sabbatical weekend resulted in the Lord addressing and walking me through Unforgiveness in my life, He did not reveal more about my next role or transition. I wrote it all down in my journal so I didn't forget one bit and would be ready to share it with Mom.

Fast forward to one week later. At about 3 am, I woke up. I asked the Lord, "is this you Lord? Did you wake me?" I heard "Yes, come with me and get your bible". I got out of bed and got my bible. I heard scripture verse after scripture verse. I kept reading wherever He took me in the Bible. After 30 minutes or so of reading scriptures about shepherds or shepherding, I heard "You are going to be a shepherd". I was bewildered at the thought. My mind raced. I was a finance and operations executive. I ran businesses. Managed and mitigated risk. Oversaw an organization for growth and profit. I had not been to seminary. All these thoughts darted through my mind. I said, "How is that possible. I don't even have a job offer." In a quick and solemn tone, I heard "I'VE JUST OFFERED THIS TO YOU!" I was like, oh, yes of course. Uhhh. Ok. Ummmmm… "Will it be at my local church?",

I asked. "Yes, but not in the traditional sense," He explained. "Okay. Wow. Thank you," I offered quietly. Then I marveled about it all and wrote it down in my journal. I finally asked God, "Is there anything else?" He tenderly replied, "No, you can go back to bed".

Shepherd: 1) one who tends sheep 2) pastor

When I woke up that Saturday morning, I couldn't wait to tell Mom what happened in the middle of the night. She was so stoked!!! We resolved to stay in prayer for further leading and waiting for God's timing. (Recall Moses was in the desert for 40 years!)

Three weeks later.

One evening after dinner as I scrolled through my email, I saw an email w the subject line "Discuss Position at Gateway Church." I did not recognize the person's name. "JENNIFER!!!" I hollered. "COME QUICKLY". I showed her the email and asked her if she has told anyone. She said no. I had not applied for the role, nor had I submitted a resume to the church. We had no idea how this person knew me or had gotten my contact info. Puzzled, but excited, we sat quietly together and read the email which included the job description. Basically, the role was financial/benevolence embedded within the Freedom Ministry. Freedom ministry was my layperson's "hobby" so to speak. And Financial was my day job! What a perfect blend of how I already spent my time. I still had no idea who this pastor was who emailed me. Never heard of her and we had attended for six years. We looked all over the church website and could not find her. Mom and I prayed. I replied and agreed to the phone interview requested in the email. The next morning, the pastor replied but asked me to come in person instead. I agreed wholeheartedly!

The interview went well. Which lead to two more interviews. The final decision maker was on a long trip to China, so I had to wait a few weeks for his interview. It would be my final interview. I was hopeful. The interview lasted 12 minutes. He only had three questions. Then asked if I had any. I also had three questions. That was it. Boom. Thanks for coming in. We'll let you know. Have a nice day. I hadn't even taken a sip of the bottled water I was given!

I was conflicted.

The interview went incredibly well. If I consider the content and connection, it went very well. Yet it was so brief. And I couldn't shake my own belief system on how brief it was. I hired and fired many people in my career. My paradigm of interviewing timeframes was simple: the less I liked you, the shorter the interview. And the more I liked you, the longer the interview. I invested more time with candidates I wanted to know and hire. My paradigm was really affecting my perception of the interview. As I walked to my car, I knew I couldn't go home. Since mom is an HR recruiter, she has a similar paradigm. I just couldn't stand to answer her questions. I drove to the lake and parked. Once I parked, I burst into tears realizing that I REALLY WANTED that role. I had other job discussions going on with law firms and investment firms, but I realized in that moment that my heart was in the pastor role. In my tears, I confessed to God that I really wanted that role. I repented of wanting what I wanted. I told God I want to want what He wants for me. And if this role is not His will, then I am ok with that and will wait for His timing.

On July 24th, I got the call and was offered the role. I accepted. I asked my hiring pastor if I could share what the Lord had told me on my sabbatical and the following week in the middle of the night. When I shared the moment God said to me, "Yes, but not in the traditional sense," she said "Oh my gosh! I just used those EXACT WORDS this morning when I described hiring for this "pastor role, but not in the traditional sense." So fun!!!

After the hiring call, I called Mom to tell her I had "a surprise for her at dinner tonight." July 24th just happened to be our 14th wedding anniversary. After the waitress took our drink order, I announced, "The church offered me the role today and I accepted!" Mom quietly responded, "It only took 14 years!" Perplexed, I questioned, "What are you talking about?" Mom went on, "Don't you remember? Before we got married, you "warned me" (with her fingers making quotations) that one day you may give up all the business and money making and go be a preacher? And you wanted to "warn me" that you had thought about giving your whole life to the Lord so if I was really caught up w all the money, etc., then maybe I better not marry you!" I was stunned. I had completely forgotten about that dream in my heart. I had let the cares of the world distract me for 14 years. We both began to cry.

God didn't forget.

He gave me the desire of my heart even when I had forgotten. And yes, I have had to humble myself in the new role. I started at the lowest pastor level at the church. I did not oversee anyone. I no longer oversaw millions of dollars in income and operations. My office had no windows. No leadership role. No strategic planning. No one asks for my thoughts or ideas or strategies. I've only gone up one pastor level all this time, and I still have a tiny office with no windows.

And guess what? The beauty of not applying, nor sending my resume is that God MADE SURE that I couldn't take credit for becoming a pastor- even if I wanted to. Lol… God did this. God offered. I accepted. I am humbled that He would allow me to serve Him by serving people. I am not able to serve as a shepherd on my own merits. God has done that and continues to do that.

MY PRAYER FOR YOU:

I pray that your dreams stay alive. I pray that you will humble yourself to the Lord in all that you do. I pray that you will acknowledge Him in you and remember that God created you with all your strengths, gifts, abilities, and great ideas! He is worthy of following because He loves you.

Go Upstairs

I know I've been sharing a lot of God moments and sharing this stuff with y'all. Most of it is pretty cool and may seem like all of them are "good moments" so to speak, on my part. Sometimes, I have conversations with God that I'm not too keen on, or fond of.

Here's one of them.

One evening, Jillienne had been either disrespectful or dishonoring and gotten out of line. Y'all know I don't tolerate that too well. Dishonoring mom or me comes with consequences. I was certainly hurt and upset, but I also stepped in to give the consequence. I don't remember all the details of the consequence, but it was more or less grounding her or losing a privilege. Of course, she was upset. I was upset. It all went down right before bedtime. I went downstairs and went to bed. Mom had already gone to sleep. I'm lying in bed and hear, "Go upstairs." I asked, "What?" "I want you to go upstairs," the Lord said. I countered, "You know what, God? No, that was the right thing. She totally disrespected me. She was not honoring us. She disobeyed. That was not right. She deserved that consequence. That's her consequence."

He said, "I want you to go upstairs." I argued, "I don't want to go. I do not want to go. That was the right thing to do. She was in the wrong. That is not okay." I was kind of arguing with God and He encouraged me, "I want you to go now." I relented, "Ah, ah, okay, fine, fine. Okay, fine. I disagree with you, but fine. I'll go back up there." So I get up and walk out of my room. (This is when we lived at Austin Oaks so you can picture the stairs) I get to the stairs and turn around to look up the stairs and there is my sweet little baby girl sitting on the top step of the stairs, bawling her eyes out.

I go to the top of the stairs, give her a hug, and we talk it out through tears. That God would love me enough to lead me to the stairs, where I was able to have a really sweet, tender moment with Jillienne is so humbling. I mean, if I didn't walk with the Lord, who knows what lies or heartache, or kind of emotional harm or father wound would've set in at that time – and possibly harmed our relationship for years. It wasn't like I felt reprimanded by God, but I certainly did not agree with what he was asking me to do. When he instructed me to go upstairs, I felt like maybe He didn't agree with what I had done. But the truth was that He knew an opportunity to reconcile was available and He was encouraging me to lay hold of it!

And you know what? It was really sweet.

I felt like God wanted me to share this testimony with y'all because not every time I'm walking and talking with the Lord is a sweet, rosy, beautiful moment. Sometimes I'm very upset. And I was pretty ticked off that time. It did not matter that the consequence was warranted. He wanted our relationship preserved! He taught me that He is a righteous God and a compassionate Father.

He's also gracious, deeply gracious. And he's merciful. And he's teaching me. He's still teaching me to stay in relationship with my kids, especially when there's a break in the trust or break in the honor or respect level, which is hurtful to me. I felt like He showed me what

He does with me. He comes closer. He basically wanted Jillienne and me to stay in relationship. He wanted us to stay close, regardless of the disagreement. I felt like God wanted me to share this with y'all so I'm not painting too rosy a picture in sharing these stories with you. I love you guys.

MY PRAYER FOR YOU:

I pray you will know that God wants to stay close even when you or I mess up, sin, or make unwise choices. I pray you will forgive me for the times I didn't come close when y'all messed up. I pray you will be brave to do God's will when you hear God guide you, especially when you feel you are in the right. I pray you will trust that God is a tender, sweet, compassionate, and loving spiritual Father who deeply desires reconciliation.

Healing Eyes

Y'all already know the outcome of the testimony with Jillienne's eyes, but I wanted to share it with you from my perspective. Y'all know Jillienne has worn glasses from the age of two or three. She got saved at age four. We went to a spirit-filled church where we saw or heard of healings. For many years, Jillienne prayed for God to heal her eyes. I would pray with her at night next to her bed asking God to heal her eyes. Even at the end of church services, she would go down front asking for prayers for God to heal her eyes.

We had many conversations, "How come God's not answering my prayer? How come God's not healing my eyes?" For the longest time I would think to myself, "Well, you know what? I mean, lots of people wear glasses their whole life. I mean this isn't cancer or something life threatening. It's just wearing glasses."

But over the years, her fervent prayer was that God would heal her eyes. When she started to lament and become deeply disappointed, I started begging God, "Would you please heal her eyes? This little kid walks with you, talks with you, knows you, trusts you, and has faith in you. Would you please heal her eyes?" I moved from a posture of yeah, she wants her eyes healed, but people wear glasses their whole life to begging God "if you know this kid, I mean, she is so enamored and loves you and believes in you and has faith. Would you please heal her eyes?"

We were still praying well into the beginning of the tween years in junior high. Then she started playing volleyball and got hit a couple of times in the face with her glasses on which cut her a little. Jillienne asked to wear contact lenses. I don't know if volleyball was the impetus or whether it was junior high peer pressure, but we got her contact lenses. And continued to pray.

A few months later, I saw her walking through the house and I said something about her contact lenses. Jillienne plainly looked at me and explained, "Well, no, I don't have to do that anymore. My eyes are healed." I stammered, "What?" She replied flatly, "Yeah, I told mom. Didn't mom tell you?" I quizzed, "No. When did you tell mom?" She chirped quickly, "'bout a month ago."

Of course, I was a little concerned that she didn't want to wear glasses anymore—junior high, discovering boys, all that kind of stuff. Jillienne said, "No Dad, they're completely healed. I can see!" But she wasn't running through the house, cheering and screaming, it was like, "Hey, it happened." I am ALL for healing, but I'm also ALL for going to the doctors and confirming the healing that you have or think you have. And that's what I told her.

We went to see the doctor.

The next available appointment was on a Monday morning. The doctor is the same doctor who has diagnosed her and treated her since she was two years old and first got glasses. 10 years with the same doctor. Monday morning was when my team meeting was scheduled at work. I told my oversight that I'd be a little late that day due to the doctor's appointment. We drove separate cars, so I could head straight to my meeting when the appointment ended. Jillienne went with Mom.

We get to the appointment and get to sit in the room as the doctor examines Jillienne's eyesight. I'll never forget the next moment in all my life! The doctor was on a swivel stool with wheels. After the examinations, he slowly turned his stool. As he turned, I saw the edge of a smile. Then I saw a big smile across his whole face- even his eyes were smiling! Our doctor is a believer too. He announced, "Yep! She's healed! 20/20 vision!" I blurted, "Oh my gosh, that is so cool! Awesome, okay, thank you very much. WOW! Gotta get to work!" I hugged everyone and left immediately. Mom and Jillienne did all the appointment checkout stuff.

It wasn't until I got to work and told everyone in the meeting that my eyes were healed, that a rush of emotion flooded me. I literally started crying in front of all my team at work as I explained what happened. I recalled all those nights that you had prayed next to your bed asking God to heal your eyes. All those times Jillienne would leave the church pew on her own, go down in front of the whole church and ask God to heal her eyes. And He finally did! I had such a rush of emotions. Heck, I'm crying right now just writing about it! It was super exciting.

The healing could not have come at a better time because not wearing glasses and seeing 20/20 certainly helped to play volleyball. A hit volleyball travels at 25-50 mph in high school. Jillienne, I know you love playing volleyball and this was a sweet, sweet gift from God. It's so sweet to see his timing and watch what he did for you, Jillienne. It's also good for our family to see the healing and the opportunity of what God can do. It was pretty awesome! Thank you for letting me share my perspective~ love y'all.

MY PRAYER FOR YOU:

I pray that each of you will recall the impact of the healing was beyond just Jillienne's eye sight. I pray you will continue to pray when you truly desire something, even for 10 years! I pray that in the lament or disappointment that you would continue to trust that God has a plan for you. I pray that you will recall that God does heal in this life!

Confess You
Stopped Trusting

This next testimony is work-related. I don't think you guys know much about this, but I wanted to share this with you. This happened when I worked as a pastor. There were some employee relations things that were not going well. I won't get into the specifics of the employee situation, but it wasn't going very well and it was difficult for me. In general, I wasn't being supported by my leadership in situations lasting over a year.

I had gotten pretty frustrated and went to HR to request a meeting with all the folks involved. I requested the meeting and then went to Hawaii for Stefen's wedding. The meeting was scheduled to be the Tuesday after we got back from Hawaii at 11:30a. Earlier that morning, I was headed to meet and interview a professional counselor in Irving. We always get to know the counselors before we recommend them to be on the church's approved counselor list.

On my way to the meeting, I was praying and worshiping in my car. I asked the Lord if there is anything He would like me to know about the meeting. He said to me, "I want you to apologize to them. When the meeting starts, I want you to apologize that you stopped trusting them in May." I inquired, "What?" He repeated, "I want you to confess that you stopped trusting them in May." This is August, mind you. I reminded God, "What? I didn't do anything wrong." And then I heard it again. He said, "I want you to confess that you stopped trusting them back in May." I relented, "Okay."

Since I was still driving, I started rehearsing in my head. "Well, I stopped trusting you back in May because you did this. And then this meeting happened, and this happened." All of a sudden, I heard, "Hey, what is that?" I wondered, "What? I was rehearsing how I would say it." I heard, "I didn't tell you to say that." I contended, "Well, I'm saying I confess that I stopped trusting you back in May because of …." And then He said, "No, no, no. That part. That's not what I told you to say." I argued, "But that's the reason I stopped trusting them, because they did this and this and this."

He said, "I understand, but I didn't tell you to say that. What I want you to say when the meeting begins, is to confess that you stopped trusting them in May, and that's it." Disappointedly, I replied, "Oh, my gosh. That's it?" He confirmed, "Yeah, that's it." I exhaled and said, "Okay, well, all right. Don't really like that, because I felt like there were some very valid reasons that I stopped trusting them, but okay, I'll do it." God had spoken, and that's what I agreed to do.

After the meeting with the counselor, I get back to the work and go into HR for the meeting. All the related parties were there. We began the meeting with prayer, then they invited me to lead the meeting since I had requested it. I began, "Well, I have something I'd like to confess." I continued, "I confess that I stopped trusting y'all back in May. Would please forgive me for that?"

My boss's boss shocked me, and said, "You had absolutely every right to stop trusting us. You don't need to apologize for that." He went on, "I need to apologize for you." He went on to list each and every reason I had been saying in the car that morning. He even shared, "it makes total sense that you had stopped trusting us." He went on to apologize for his part and asked for forgiveness as well.

Man, that meeting changed in an instant! He was crying. I was crying. It was amazing! The humbling of ourselves and submitting ourselves one to another. Right outta the Word of God! It was pretty awesome, beautiful and holy.

I wanted to share this with you so you could see God's ability to change things for the good when we listen to Him. I called that meeting because I felt that things were not going well and that I was being maligned. It was for a good and righteous reason! The Lord knew what needed to happen, and more importantly, HOW it needed to happen. Even when He told me what to say, I didn't want to say it the way He wanted me to say it. I wanted to list all the reasons that I stopped trusting them. God basically reprimanded me gently but firmly. He said, "That's it. That's all I want you to say."

The meeting gave me the opportunity to say what needed to be said. It gave my oversights the opportunity to say what he needed to say, and there was reconciliation and restoration. It was really powerful and cool and amazing. And even the HR director said something like, "I don't think I've ever been in a meeting like this before. This was clearly a move of the Holy Spirit. This was just amazing to witness. I would like to pray and thank God for what I just witnessed." And we did.

I want to share with you that even after I called the meeting and kept moving closer to it, the Lord had a way that He wanted it to go. Had I not followed His way, it would have been very different, I'm sure. God's ways work. I felt like that was an important God moment to share with y'all. Since that time, there was an amazing restoration of that relationship. I'm still friends with the guy in the meeting that also confessed and apologized to me. We forgave each other. It's been pretty cool ever since.

MY PRAYER FOR YOU:

I pray that you will strive to live in righteousness and submission to God even when believers around you mess up. I pray you will be gracious with brother and sisters in Christ just as God is with you. I pray you will allow God room and time to work on someone's heart just as He gives works on your heart. I pray you will be willing to see your part in situations and be courageous enough to ask God how He wants you to handle it.

I Am Your Provider

On a long drive through west Texas and New Mexico desert tundra, our car lost all the oil about 2 miles outside the village of Des Moines, New Mexico- a town of 128 people. Fortunate for us, Des Moines happens to have a gas station, a mechanic, and a 5-room motel. We rolled into the "auto shop" which looked more like parking outside a barn, and got out to find the mechanic. When I asked the mechanic if he could take a look at my car and see how it lost all the oil, he responds "Sure, but it will probably take a few days for me to fix it because we only go into town 1-2 times per week for parts. So you'll have to stay at the M&M Inn next door." Not exactly the best news since we are on our way to pack up and bring our college daughter home from a university in Colorado. Which, by the way, we were notified two days prior that the college campus will close the following day at 5p due to the Coronavirus! So we were in a bit of a hurry. I kindly replied, "Thank you," and then shared the news with mom, who was still in the car. While I was standing outside the vehicle, mom gets out to join me and begins to tell me through tears that we need to ask angels to tend to us and that we need to ask God to intervene somehow. I smiled, and replied in my most positive tone, "I'm pretty sure God has ALREADY taken care of us- we have driven stretches of the panhandle with no towns for 30-50 miles in either direction.

The warning light and bell went off just a mile before this town. The town has a gas station, a mechanic, and a place to stay!!! I'd say God has hooked us up ALREADY!" She then reminds me through her tears, "What about our daughter in Colorado? What's she gonna do?" I put my arm around her and we prayed. Soon thereafter I heard Ryan (the mechanic) ask me if Toyota made my type of car (which was a Lexus). Ryan continued that they don't see many hybrid cars "in these parts", and then said he can't read the language in the engine so do I "know how big my engine is?" With all the doubt those questions brought to my mind, the next 15 minutes revealed how much MORE God had ALREADY moved on our behalf.

In short order, Ryan diagnoses the problem and realizes that he had actually picked up a part that morning for "Marla's" car. And that part for Marla's car would fit our car. (I don't know who Marla is but I'm excited that she unknowingly was donating her car part to my car). Ryan asks me what type of oil my car takes. I answer that my car takes 0-20 synthetic oil. He shakes his head and says "I'll be right back". Ryan returns and shares that he has five quarts of the 0-20 synthetic oil which is "practically miraculous" (his words) because not that many vehicles need that type of oil in Des Moines, New Mexico! Through each of these amazing discoveries, we keep saying "That is SO GOD", "Thank you GOD", "GOD is so good"- and the mechanic, and his Dad who came up to help, kept saying "Yup", "He is" and "Sure is". We could all see how truly remarkable the situation was as it unfolded moment by moment. Forty-five minutes later, we paid the bill, blessed Ryan, and drove off.

God provides. God sees to it. Jehovah Jireh.

It doesn't end there. As I drove off, I heard "No matter how much you plan, how much money you have, how good your car is, I am your provider." I burst into tears. You see, I had spent a great deal of time planning the trip and the possible contingencies. I had removed a very large sum of cash from the bank in case banks went offline during our trip. We drove our most reliable vehicle for the trip. Yet, God knew that I needed a reminder in the midst of all the chaos, noise, and stress of that day, AND, that I will need it for the days ahead (this was the beginning of Covid). He knows what I need and moves mightily to SHOW ME that He is at work ALREADY on my behalf.

And your behalf as well.

God Provides. God Sees To It.

Jehovah Jireh

MY PRAYER FOR YOU:

I pray that you will plan your best, yet trust God for He is the provider. I pray that you will know that in the midst of very huge worldwide events which seem disheartening, God is with you. I pray that when you begin to rely on your money, education, reliable car, or whatever is not God, you will hear His gentle reminder that He provides. I pray you will remember Jehovah Jireh is a name of God which means "The Lord Sees To It."

The Decade Is Not Over

This God moment conversation happened much more recently and is the primary impetus to producing Stacking Stones with all the God moment testimonials that I'm sharing with you.

I know you know I had three surgeries in the Fall of 2021. I had the bone graft in my jaw, which was an emergency surgery, on September 7th. The very next week, September 14th, I had surgery that had already been scheduled a couple of months in advance. It was for the repair of the labrum and some other things in my shoulder. Then on October 9th, I had kidney stone surgery. Three surgeries in about six weeks. It was a painful and difficult run of it. I know y'all know about that.

I want to share some details about the third surgery that lead to conversations with the Lord which changed my life.

When I arrived at the hospital early on a Saturday, I was in excruciating pain. Mind you, I'm already taking Hydrocodone every six hours a day for my shoulder pain! The doctors immediately treat me with Dilaudid in an attempt to reduce the pain. Throughout the day, I was suffering through bouts of excruciating pain and nausea for about 8 hours. After some tests, the doctor had come in to explain what had happened, what was going on with my body, and what the surgery plans will be. He spoke continuously until he got all his information out, so to speak. In the middle of his detailed analysis, he made the comment, "Well, you stopped breathing on us and your blood pressure dropped into the 30s. So we needed to get you back." Even though he kept speaking. I didn't hear any of it.

He lost me at "you stopped breathing."

I mean, I'm already doped up on the three doses of Dilaudid I received that day. I've been on painkillers for about a month at this point. I honestly didn't hear anything past the part where he said, "You stopped breathing and your blood pressure dropped into the 30s." I've watched enough doctor TV shows to know when the blood pressure drops that low, they start screaming, "Clear!" so they can shock someone's heart into action! They're trying to get someone back whose heart is crashing. I was kind of in shock. When the doctor leaves, I look at mom and I ask, "Hey, did that doctor say I stopped breathing?" Mom whispered, "Yeah." I continued, "And the whole blood pressure dropping under 30 thing. Did he say that too?" Quietly, mom replied "Yeah." I inquired, "Well, have you been here the whole time?" Mom confirmed, "Yeah." I quizzed, "Did you know any of that?" She shrugged and said, "No." It was an eye-opening moment for me. I think to myself, "Wow. I have a kidney stone and I almost die? That's nuts, right?"

So that stuck with me.

I had surgery. It went fine. I went home. It was crazy painful the following days. I think they either tore or agitated my urethra. It was very, very painful to go number one. It was so painful that I was crying and screaming at the same time when I went. It was burning and so painful. I was crying for days. In the week following the third surgery, I was crying out to God begging him, "Please. No more surgeries, nothing else. I've had three in six weeks. Please, Lord. Please, can you stop them? I know you have the ability. Can you please stop these?"

I heard, "Well, what about you?"

That doesn't sound very compassionate. I queried, "What?" I heard Him again, "You haven't stewarded your body. These surgeries are your doing." I was stunned by the clarity. In an instant, I thought about each surgery. The bone graft in the jaw- that had to do with me not taking care of something my dentist recommended. The shoulder injury- I had not worked out in many years, then started working out during Covid and hurt myself. The kidney stone- my kidney doctor has asked me to do an analysis which determines foods to avoid that cause stones. I had not done that either. All those memories went through my mind in a flash. I knew that was God's voice and I knew He was right. I humbly confessed, "Oh my gosh, that's true. You're right. You're right. I'm the one who hasn't stewarded my body well at all."

The next thing which came to mind at that moment was a conversation back in May of 2016, when the Lord had said to me, "Hey, I'm going to need you to get healthy for this next decade. The things I have for you, I'm going to need you to be healthy to do it." God reminded me of that moment. I confessed, "Oh my gosh, that's right. I remember that." I turned 50 in August of 2016. In May 2016 as God requested, I started getting healthy, working out, and running. I turned 50 feeling pretty healthy and was excited about the decade of my 50s. Three weeks later, I was diagnosed with cancer. Boom.

I'd forgotten his encouragement and instruction. I'd forgotten all about that conversation. I'd forgotten about God encouraging me to be healthy. I'd forgotten about His plans for my decade. In the moment that I was repenting for not taking care of my body, the Lord showed me the conversation in May 2016 in a snap. I remember saying to God,

"Oh my gosh, Lord. Yeah, I forgot all about that." He encouraged me, "Well, the decade's not over." I grinned. Then I chuckled. Then He asked, "Do you want to get well?" "YES, I DO!!!" I proclaimed.

I knew that meant more than getting healthy. I felt like what he was also inviting me to repent, to change my mind, to actually come and follow him in His way of health. So right then and there, I said, "Okay. I repent. I change my mind. I repent for not taking care of my body. I want to steward my body and take care of it. It's my body, but your temple, Lord, and I want to take care of it for you." As soon as I repented and said that to the Lord, I realized, "I don't know how to take care of my body." I have not done a very good job. I've been bouncing between about 220 to 250 pounds for 20 something years- up and down, up and down. Even 220 is not a healthy weight for me. An optimum weight would be more like 195-200.

I confessed, "Gosh, God, I don't know how to take care of my body. I mean, I'm going to need your help. Will you please help me?" I heard, "Yes." The pain subsided and healing came. I prayed daily for wisdom and His help in being healthy. I began paying attention to eating more fruits and vegetables and paying attention to the nutrition. I did really well for about 10 days. Until I found myself on a Saturday night standing in front of the refrigerator eating sweets. When it dawns on me what I'm doing, I say out loud, "God! What is going on? What is happening?" I heard, "You are hurting." My first response was, "Well, of course I'm hurting. I had three surgeries." He urged, "No, you're H U R T I N G," kind of long and deep, the way He said it. And I was standing at the fridge thinking, "Hurting? Hurting?" Then I remembered. Earlier that morning, Stefen and I had gotten in kind of a text argument.

For a few weeks, I had been trying to arrange a time to talk with him about how I felt he had dishonored me. He probably didn't do it on purpose, but I wanted to talk to him about it. He totally blew me off and acted like I was irrational. Stefen had a "You're just overreacting" kind of posture toward me. Even in the text conversation, he still dishonored me by not allowing me to share how I feel about it. I was hurt and upset. And here I was standing at the fridge, realizing that I am hurting and angry. I started bawling right there at the fridge. God was right. I was hurting and I wasn't doing very well. As I stood there crying, the Lord gently and tenderly said "You do this sometimes with your emotions when you're hurting. You come and eat to comfort yourself. I want to be your comforter." I began to cry even harder when I heard that. In the midst of my tears, He tenderly shared, "And you do this sometimes with your work." And I thought, "Oh my God." As a counseling pastor, people tell you some really horrific things that they've endured, or they've committed. It can be some emotional stuff. As soon as he said that about work, I thought, "Oh, no. I love doing that. I want to be able to keep helping people." So I implored, "Lord, I'm going to need you to help me with this. I want you to be my comforter. So please, please help me." He agreed.

One of the names for the Holy Spirit in the Bible is "the Great Comforter." That night at the fridge was a wake-up call. It was huge to realize that comforting myself was weak and didn't honor one of the Holy Spirit's roles in my life. It was a cool moment with God to learn to invite him into my pain or my sadness. You know, the people that you're closest to, Stefen in this case, are going to hurt you the most because they are the people with whom you are most vulnerable. That was a big realization about 10 days after the last surgery! I loved that God was wonderfully candid with me about the poor stewardship of my body when I was begging for no more surgeries. Then, to have Him bring to my mind a conversation from 2016 was so loving and kind.

Interestingly, the first time the Lord told me to share some of my God moments with you was after He led me through cancer. And here I am six years later- He's leading me, guiding me, showing me how to be healthy. He's showing me how to take care of myself, steward what he wants for my body, and leading me into new directions he wants me to pursue.

The decade's not over! I'm going to pursue Him and the things He has deposited in me to share with and offer to the Body of Christ!

I love y'all.

MY PRAYER FOR YOU:

I pray that even in your deepest pain you will reach out to God. I pray you will forgive me for not stewarding my body well for many years and for the poor example I gave you in relation to your own bodies. I pray you will know that God loves you and makes plans for you! I pray you will know that God is strong, that He is tender, and that He will sustain you with His strong right arm. I pray you will know that I am endeavoring to follow God wholeheartedly and to fulfill His purpose for my life on earth. And I pray that each of you will know how much I love, admire, and appreciate you!